"John Davis is indeed a tender but strong warrior, as well as one of the most gifted people I have ever known. His giftedness has shown once again in *Extreme Pursuit*, which is informative, practical, and personable. A must-read."

— FRANK MINIRTH, MD, PhD

"John Davis captures the heart of a father and provides the wisdom much needed for dad's raising sons in the twenty-first century! Within today's culture, it's an entirely different ballpark for the father-son relationship. *Extreme Pursuit* motivates men to turn the challenge into victory with an applicable winning strategy!"

— DR. JOE WHITE, president, Kanakuk Kamps

Extreme Pursuit

Winning the Race for the Heart of Your Son

JOHN E. DAVIS, M.A.

NAVPRESS®

BRINGING TRUTH TO LIFE

OUR GUARANTEE TO YOU

We believe so strongly in the message of our books that we are making this quality guarantee to you. If for any reason you are disappointed with the content of this book, return the title page to us with your name and address and we will refund to you the list price of the book. To help us serve you better, please briefly describe why you were disappointed. Mail your refund request to: NavPress, P.O. Box 35002, Colorado Springs, CO 80935.

The Navigators is an international Christian organization. Our mission is to advance the gospel of Jesus and His kingdom into the nations through spiritual generations of laborers living and discipling among the lost. We see a vital movement of the gospel, fueled by prevailing prayer, flowing freely through relational networks and out into the nations where workers for the kingdom are next door to everywhere.

NavPress is the publishing ministry of The Navigators. The mission of NavPress is to reach, disciple, and equip people to know Christ and make Him known by publishing life-related materials that are biblically rooted and culturally relevant. Our vision is to stimulate spiritual transformation through every product we publish.

ISBN-13: 978-1-60006-100-4
ISBN-10: 1-60006-100-1

Cover design by The DesignWorks Group, Inc, David Uttley, www.thedesignworksgroup.com
Cover image by Getty
Creative Team: Terry Behimer, Traci Mullins, Reagen Reed, Arvid Wallen, Pat Reinheimer
Author photo by Valerie Davis

Some of the anecdotal illustrations in this book are true to life and are included with the permission of the persons involved. All other illustrations are composites of real situations, and any resemblance to people living or dead is coincidental.

Published in association with the literary agency of Alive Communications, Inc., 7680 Goddard Street, Suite 200, Colorado Springs, CO 80920 (www.alivecommunications.com).

Davis, John E., 1968-
  Extreme pursuit : winning the race for the heart of your son / John E. Davis.
    p. cm.
  Includes bibliographical references.
  ISBN-13: 978-1-60006-100-4
  ISBN-10: 1-60006-100-1
  1. Parent and teenager--Religious aspects--Christianity. 2. Teenage boys--Religious life. I. Title.
BV4529.D37 2007
248.8'45--dc22
                                2007009954

Printed in the United States of America

1 2 3 4 5 6 7 8 / 11 10 09 08 07

FOR A FREE CATALOG OF NAVPRESS BOOKS & BIBLE STUDIES,
CALL 1-800-366-7788 (USA) OR 1-800-839-4769 (CANADA).

For my Dad
I love you

Table of Contents

Foreword

I am a licensed professional counselor. I counsel adolescents (mostly girls) and their families. I have even written a few parenting books for mothers and their teenage daughters. I am always looking for resources to support my work in this area.

Years ago a pastor told me about John Davis. He said, "If you ever need to make a referral to a counselor for an adolescent boy, I recommend John." I started referring inquiring parents (mostly moms) to John. And then something remarkable happened. I started hearing back from these same moms. They said things like:

> "Thank you for sending us to John. He saved my son's life!"
>
> "Thank you for telling us about John. He's changing our entire family."
>
> "Thank you for knowing about John. He is just what we needed."

I make a lot of referrals, but I seldom get follow-up phone calls like this, so I decided I needed to meet this man. I invited him for coffee at Starbucks. John showed up carrying his Nalgene water bottle (he didn't drink coffee, which worried me a little, because Starbucks is important to me!). He exuded health and passion. I knew that I was meeting a rare man. He told me about his adolescence, a story of excellence in athletics and loneliness in relationships. He disclosed his mistakes in looking for connection in all the wrong places. He talked about the million little pieces of brokenness in him that led him to some extreme places. And then he told me of his passion for helping boys who are lost in a culture that sucks them into dark and dangerous places and whose parents don't know how to find and help them. I was hooked. I knew that John would be my "referral" for as long as he practiced.

What I didn't know was that two years later my own family would fall apart. A messy, unthinkable divorce. And I had a fourteen-year-old son who was quickly becoming one of the lost boys John had talked about. My son had low self-esteem, an absentee dad, and a mom who didn't know what a teenage boy needed. You can guess who I called: John Davis.

When we met again I told him my story—of my own failures, my ex-husband's failures, and my son's struggles with self-esteem, depression, and experimentation with drugs. (Who would blame him for wanting something to make him feel better in the midst of the mess his parents had created?) I was nervous. I knew that I, the counselor, writer, "expert on adolescents," had made a big mess of things.

After I'd told John my story, I showed him my son's eighth-grade picture. John didn't lecture or advise. He cried. He looked at the picture of my son—an awkward, confused, lonely boy—and he cried for him. *I need you to get this.* This big, athletic, handsome, competent man wept for my lost boy!

And then John said, "Sharon, I don't know exactly how to help your son. But I *can* help him. And you are not alone. Let me take it from here."

Single mom (or mom in a marriage feeling like a single mom), you "get" how these were words of life to me. John gave me an extravagant gift for which I owe a debt of gratitude I can never repay. If you are a single mom or a mom doing most of the parenting on your own, this book is for you! You might read about some mistakes you've made. We moms don't know how to relate perfectly to our sons. They are "other." John can give you powerful tools as well as encourage you to invite your son's dad to participate more fully in his life.

During our counseling with John, he said to my son and me that the whole point of the counseling was to transfer what John offered to my son to the healing of his relationship with his dad. I hated that because I was early in the process of forgiving his father. My son hated it because he didn't want his dad at that time. But John was right. My son and his father have forged a healthy relationship that is guiding my now-eighteen-year-old son to being a man—something a boy can learn *only* from his father.

And so, dads, this book is for you! You may feel guilty for your choices or inadequate to guide your son or emasculated by your wife's criticisms of you, but *you* are what your son needs to be the man he was created to be. I know of no one better than John to help you with that. He passionately wants to give you tools to help your son. He can do it if you will acknowledge that you can't do it without help.

My son's time in therapy with John was short-lived, due to circumstances beyond our control. In our final session, once again John said very little. He wept. He cried in front of my son because of his sorrow that they would no longer be seeing each other every week. Months later on occasions of failure and success, my son would ask me, "Can I call John and tell him about this?" John is tough—a little. But he is mostly tender—full of fierce compassion for his adolescent clients. And they love him because he loves them. And that really is the key.

John can teach you to be tough. That might hurt at times because facing our failures or oversights is humbling. But John can also teach you to be tender. I've seen him cry much more than "kick butt." Moms and dads, he'll teach you to be tough and tender in the midst of pain, disgust, confusion, fear, and agony. And then you'll be what your teenage boy needs—a rare parent for a boy who is no ordinary boy.

John Davis is a strong man who climbs mountains; confronts abusive parents; counsels teenagers who hide guns, sell drugs, or get hooked by pornography. He's a man who heads straight into all that most of us want to look away from. So if your son is three and just starting to talk a blue streak, read this book. If your son is thirteen and wanting a tattoo, read this book. If your son is seventeen and using drugs, read this book. If your son is twenty-three and living in a dark hole away from you and God, read this book. It's never too late to begin an extreme pursuit for the heart of your son.

Thank you, John, for weeping for my son and me. You are a tender warrior. We parents have a lot to learn from you.

Sharon A. Hersh, M.A.
Lone Tree, Colorado

1

The Chase Is On

In December 2001 I took a group of guys on a mountaineering expedition to Longs Peak—a 14,259-foot mountain near Estes Park, Colorado. We spent a day mountaineering, which included ice climbing, building a snow igloo, and working together as a team on a safety rope. That night, however, we experienced an unexpected wicked prewinter storm accompanied by extreme winds and below-zero temperatures. We had all the appropriate gear and were *generally* prepared—except for the *extreme* change in weather. That night the temperature was minus twenty degrees.

The following morning the gas tanks for our cooking stoves were frozen, so we couldn't boil snow for water and couldn't cook breakfast. Everyone ate trail mix while we shivered in the poststorm cold. I went out to warm up the tanks in the sun and take photos of our snow igloos. While taking pictures, I noticed another dramatic change in the climate. Clouds poured off the diamond face of the mountain, cascading and rolling over the peaks and into our campsite. I yelled at everyone to get ready for another storm! Within three minutes winds hit in excess of eighty miles per hour and tore through our gear, throwing it in every direction for more than eight hundred feet. I could barely stay standing.

After the storm had blown through, about three hours later, we gathered and packed our gear and climbed down. Our tents were torn, and the risk in staying was too great, as I noticed yet another front that would no doubt bring with it more treacherous wind and snow. We didn't make the summit, but everyone was alive.

How many parents feel like a storm is coming? Some do. Maybe that's why you picked up this book. You sense that things are off; the barometer that you use to read your son is telling you that something is coming over the horizon, maybe before you're ready. Many parents don't anticipate a storm because their kid seems "well-enough behaved"—for a teenager, anyway. He's keeping up in school, playing sports, even going to church youth group. They don't know a storm is already brewing behind the diamond-like facade. Their son may be experimenting with drugs, abusing alcohol, or having sex—all while the climate seems pretty balmy.

Caught Unawares

At sixteen Garrett was creative, bright, and popular with his peers. He maintained a 3.75 grade point average and held down a regular job. The first sign that things might not be as they appeared was Garrett's first misdemeanor: possession of marijuana. His second encounter with the law came because he liked to go joyriding around his neighborhood in his truck. One evening he ran over three trees, valued at more than $1,800, which he paid to have replaced. His third cry for attention came when he got arrested for driving under the influence, blowing a .245, which is about four times the legal limit. This time he drove into a burning campfire. His fourth collision with the law was a misdemeanor—a minor-in-possession-of-alcohol ticket, considered by many teenagers as a badge of honor. His fifth scream for attention came when he was flagged over by police officers. Knowing that he was driving without a license, Garrett tried to flee the police. His sixth attempt to get someone to notice what was going on inside him came when he drove intoxicated to his scheduled probation appointment.

You might be thinking—where were his parents? Were they even in the same country? Well, you would have wanted to ask my parents the same thing if you had known me twenty-five years ago. I was attending high school, although I participated as minimally as I could. I was involved in sports and extracurricular activities, and I had a few close friends. My parents asked me the questions that parents should be asking. Despite my parents' and siblings' efforts to relate to me, however, I was an angry kid. I was sensitive to criticism and defensive about personal growth and change. I made a lot of bad choices as a result of feeling emotionally disconnected, and I couldn't understand (any more than my parents could) why I resisted what I most craved—connection with others.

Garrett told me once, "My dad was so disappointed in me. He never really yelled, though, except when I showed up at the house drunk. Normally, he would put his hand on his forehead and shake his head and say, 'When are you going to learn?'

"I kept on making dumb choices based on the fact that I really wanted to fit in. It was huge for me to see my dad devastated. But after I'd have a month of good behavior, I'd forget about his disappointing looks. I always got way ahead of myself, feeling that nothing would get in the way of my success."

After working together for six months, Garrett and I were able to determine that he was operating on a six-week cycle emotionally. His acting out was tied directly to his emotions. Garrett would have three to four weeks of success and be feeling really great about himself, and then a buildup of emotions that he wasn't working through would trip him into a downward spiral. This really hit him hard. Garrett was sensitive and had a sweet disposition, but this internal struggle was tearing him apart from the inside out, and his choices reflected that. Many times in our sessions Garrett would express tremendous frustration and self-contempt. We spent hours talking about every behavior he had ever tried in order to help turn himself around and be the best young man he could be, but it took us about a year of individual and family counseling to find the keys to this boy's heart.

Extreme Times Call for Extreme Measures

These are extreme days. The media and electronic technologies have accelerated and amplified *everything*. Things happen earlier, faster, and with more intensity than ever before. Adolescence is no exception. This stage of human development has always been unmatched by any other in terms of its rapid physical changes, roller-coaster emotions, and relational turmoil. It is crucial that we match these extreme days with an extreme pursuit of our sons.

Today's boys are engaging in higher levels of extreme behavior than ever before. Boys as young as nine are immersed in pornography and substance abuse. Even boys who are not engaged in extreme behaviors are influenced by peers and media that suggest that these behaviors define masculinity. The behaviors of teenage boys reveal an internal wiring that drives them to be extraordinary, to build something great, to create an impact on their world—rather than to be average, left alone, unchallenged, and uninspired.

At a time when boys need strong, appropriate modeling, many parents are disconnected from their sons because of the demands of their own lives and their perceived inability to make a difference in their son's world. One of my friends told me that when she saw her sons' school's number on their caller ID, she wouldn't answer. We're all tempted to put our heads in the sand or look the other way and hope it's not *our* son who will get into trouble. But it's not worth the risk because the risks out there are huge. Disengaged parents usually find out much too late that they should have been doing more, and in many cases, what they were doing should have been done differently. The world can be a dark and dangerous place for a boy.

Over the past decade I've counseled more than a thousand boys and young men. They fit what may be a surprising profile to many, in that they are bright and have sensitive hearts. Almost without exception, however, *they are emotionally disconnected.* Their souls are adrift, with no anchor for stability or harbor for protection, and the world eats them up. In many cases, by the time a parent is alert to the danger, a tremendous amount of damage has already been done. That's usually when I get the call—an anxious, frustrated parent is seeing their son being devoured and they don't know how to stop it.

As a teen your son is desperately searching for his own identity as he interacts with the world. Teens seek *experiences* and will gravitate to people who fit into that experiential mindset, a mindset that asks, "How do I really connect with the world?" They look for answers in girls, sports, parties, academics, or withdrawal into a private world of their own music, video games, and computer interactions. A son in this phase is likely to abandon anything that can't help him answer the question, "How do I really connect?" In short, teen boys are desperately trying to find themselves *and* remain connected to someone. Often boys will give up things that are important (values, hobbies, interests, beliefs) in an effort to connect somewhere.

Boys who are in trouble are emotionally disconnected in some important ways from the people most essential to helping them find their identity. They are on the run, looking for something or someone to give them direction as well as relationship that meets the deepest needs of their heart. I understand it's hard to stay connected to a sullen, angry, awkward—sometimes even scary—adolescent boy. Many parents of teenage sons are desperately seeking skills and a strategy. If that sounds like you, be encouraged. I'll help you find both. For example, do you know why "shoulder-to-shoulder" communication is better than "face-to-face" with a teenage boy? Do you know the things that repel your son rather than draw him to you? The answers to those questions and many more are in the chapters ahead. You *can* learn to effectively communicate and connect with your son in this volatile phase of his life. I'll give you principles and practical ideas that will empower you to both "get it" and "do it."

I find that dads, especially, need tools. I will give you new tools and I'll coach you in more effectively using the tools you already have. Of the 133 sons I have on my client list right now, only five of their dads are actively engaged with their sons. Usually I get calls from moms looking for solutions, desperate for help. Being a dad is a responsibility, but it's also an opportunity—a chance to be a part of something huge, something that's going to outlast anything else you do. You have an opportunity to get a front-row seat and watch a boy being transformed into a man. You have the chance to rise to the occasion and face one of the most daunting challenges on the planet because you have a son and you're his dad. When you engage in pursuing relationship with him and begin to see even the *slightest* bit of progress, you'll know you've had the privilege to be a part of something more important than anything else you've ever done or ever will do.

Mom, I suspect you're tired of lugging the toolbox around. You've tried using the tools and feel like they're not working. That could be because they're not the tools you're supposed to be using. I'm going to give you permission to hand the toolbox over to your son's father. If you're in this parenting thing alone, I'll coach you as to which tools to use and how to use them effectively in a boy's life. You *can* parent your son with skill and grace.

A Race You Need to Win

I suspect that whether you're a mom or a dad, you picked up this book because something inside you is leading you toward a more strategic, empowered pursuit of relationship with your son. Something has motivated you to make it a priority at this time. Do you know what it is? What's the dream? What's the crisis? What's the need you are feeling deep down inside? In my experience you're probably in one of the following situations.

Your son has "disappeared." You thought you knew who he was. You thought you knew where he was, and you may have even thought you knew where he was going. But something changed. He is *physically* present in your home (to the extent that he empties out the refrigerator every night), but it's like a fog has descended and *you've lost contact.*

You are in crisis. Things have started to unravel and are headed in the wrong direction. Rules are being broken. Conversations are overrun by anger and harsh words. Perhaps you found pornography on the computer or marijuana in his sock drawer. The police or the principal has called. He's breaking stuff and hitting people. You suspect he's sleeping with his girlfriend. Life is coming apart at the seams and *you don't know what to do.*

Seasons are changing. Time moves very quickly, and you might be watching the years slip away—watching your son slip away—through the one-way doors of time that can never be reentered. There is a desire deep inside of you—one that is often drowned out in the noise and demands of daily details; but deep in your soul *you want to connect with him before it's too late*—and you see that opportunity passing by with each passing day.

Wherever you find yourself, you've made a decision to *do* something to capture the heart of your son. You're in hot pursuit—or you want to be, but how do you know which direction to run? Certain strategies work, others don't. When we are just hanging on for dear life, winging it as best we can, we miss strategic opportunities to go after our sons with passionate pursuit and tactical maneuvers that really work.

The chase is on and it's a chase like no other. It's a pursuit of something vitally important to you, to your family, and to our world. In many ways the chase is also a race. A race against time. A race against evil. It is a race you *need* to win, for it is *a race for the heart of a son*, your son, no matter where he is and no matter where he is headed.

The pursuit of your son is one of incalculable significance, but it is a daunting and difficult one. If you're feeling beat up and scared, you may be reluctant to pick up the chase. If you're feeling rejected and hurt, you may not want to open yourself up to more pain. If you're feeling angry and resentful, you may be ready to flush everything and abandon the race all together. But you will feel better as you do something new that begins to make a difference. If you take up the chase in the ways I'm going to suggest in the pages ahead, it will mean great reward for you and your son, even though it might look totally different for your family than you anticipated or hoped for. If you pursue your son's heart, there will be moments when you will capture it and connect with it in ways you never dreamed possible. And that's about as amazing as it gets.

Whether it's for the thousandth time or for the first time, now is the time to begin an extreme pursuit for the heart of your son, a pursuit that is equal to the extreme world that will try to take him captive. Time is slipping away. You can waste it or you can give it another shot and make it count for something important, like your son's heart. Your own heart is telling you that it's time to take action, step up, do something, right now, with the hope that it will make a difference for your son, your family, and our world. My promise to you is to give you specific, concrete ideas. I'm asking you to try it, or try it again. Risk again. Be willing to be hurt again, because pursuing your son's heart is worth getting hurt, looking like a fool, and bumbling through changes that may feel awkward or questionable at first.

As you begin your pursuit, you will naturally want to see results. But I urge you to stay focused on the chase because it's all about the process. You might be very disappointed—maybe even devastated—over how things are turning out with your son. You might be dealing with regret, longing to rewrite the past or do it over again. You might be wondering how to make the very best of the days ahead. It's easy to get fixated on changing your circumstances or correcting a problem, but to win this race you must focus on the *relationship*, on capturing the *heart* of your son. What lies ahead is a journey, not a destination, and the ride could very well be a wild one. There will be encouragement and light, but the road will undoubtedly have dips and ruts. The valleys into which you descend may be dark — *really* dark. Great hope exists, but in the shadows enemies lurk, and any one of them may trip you up, or cause your son to fall after he's stood tall for some time. If you focus on the results, it's going to be a roller coaster. If you focus on the process, you will be amazed at the view, and the journey will blow you away.

In a therapy session with Garrett two years into the process, we were discussing what his choices had "cost" him along the way. A week later he brought in a T-shirt he'd created to wear to his homecoming football game. On the front of the shirt in huge bold print was ".245." At the bottom of the shirt in smaller print it said "GPA? No, DUI!" On the back of the shirt he listed the following costs, hoping to encourage sobriety among his classmates.

Court Costs:	$500
Ankle Monitor:	$1,200
Community Service:	$600
Therapy:	$9,200
Breathalyzers:	$400
Urine Testing:	$1,400
Probation:	$1,000
Replacing Trees:	$1,800
Loss of Vehicle:	$7,500
Total cost:	$23,600
Lessons learned:	Priceless!

You have a lot invested in your son too. Time, money, and emotion to name a few. Add to that the skills you will learn in the pages ahead and the commitment you bring to the table, and it will all add up to a process that is priceless.

Steady yourself and take a deep breath, because the pursuit of your son's heart is a journey of heroic proportions. I applaud you for your courage and determination — no matter how often they may falter. I will give you every resource I know to win the race. *The chase is on.*

GO FOR IT!

ON YOUR MARKS!

Take fifteen minutes and write out the top five ways in which you would like to connect better with your son. Keep your list free from things you want your son to do. Focus on what you can do to improve or create the relationship.

GET SET!

Draw up a list of what you think you may have to do to make this happen. Spend some time looking at your own issues and reflecting on how your son's responses have kept you out of his world.

GO!

You hold the key to open the door of communication and connection with your son. If you are not sure where to start, leave a blank to be filled in later, but be sure to come back and make note of specific things you can do as you learn new skills. Use the following chapters to construct a plan for winning the race for your son's heart.

2

Kid Repellent

When a boy starts getting hair under his armpits and his feet start smelling, you know that significant changes are coming your way. As early as age twelve your "little" boy enters a stage of unprecedented cognitive, physical, and psychosocial development—all without your "permission"—or his!

For starters your son now has more intense and more impulsive brain activity. He's thinking, defining, figuring things out on his own. He sees the world beyond home, begins to question almost everything, and thinks he might want to try almost anything. You see him thinking, but you can't see *what* he's thinking—and he may not tell you. Actually, he may not even be *able* to tell you what he's thinking. When he says over and over and over again, "I don't know," he may actually be telling the truth. Did *you* understand your own thoughts when you were that age?

Second, your son has a changing body, a body that is strong—perhaps stronger than yours—and injected with hormones telling it to do all sorts of crazy things.

Third, your boy will soon have the keys to the car. With age comes mobility, making it more and more difficult to keep track of where he is. All this adds up to a life that is infinitely more complex. Parenting your son when he was younger was like playing checkers; now you're playing chess. The strategies are much more complicated. In fact, the strategies that you used in the earlier years don't work on teens, and in many cases only annoy them. A whole new set of principles for pursuing the heart of your son needs to be understood and put into practice.

When I work with adolescent boys and their families, I often use metaphors from the climbing and mountaineering world for the parent-child relationship as well as for the child's relationships with himself and the rest of the world. When boys and their parents begin to navigate the ups and downs of adolescence, they are often climbing some pretty steep mountains and having to rappel down some heart-pounding cliffs to return to safety. Most parents aren't even fully conscious of the dynamics that begin to develop between parent and child as they enter into the unfamiliar landscape of adolescence. Often, when parents see a conflict or disturbance coming toward them in the form of their son, before they know it, without even realizing it, out of fear, panic, disgust, or confusion, they hold up their arm and motion with their hand or voice for their son to "Stop!" This response is normal. We've been doing it since they started crawling. We see a child move toward something dangerous or out of bounds and we yell, grab, or motion for him to "Stop," reminding him of danger and consequences.

The upright palm in the face of a child may be appropriate in the younger years, but as boys enter preadolescence, they naturally begin to form a new response in the face of the "stop sign" before them. Most boys have been thinking about it for a while—filing away the experiences of being told "Stop!" or "Don't do that!" or "Don't even think about it." Their developing adolescent brains have been telling them to question, think about it, come to their own conclusions; but the hand in their face tells them the opposite: "Don't ask questions. Don't think. Do as you are told, no matter what you think or feel."

Yikes! What a position this puts growing boys in. They either shut down to their own questions and swirling emotions, or they shut down to their parents, who they feel are basically telling them, "Don't tell me what you think or want. Just *stop*." Because most teenage boys *want* a relationship with their parents, they are caught in a dilemma that is past their ability at this developmental stage to solve. They don't want to shut down their evolving inner world, and they don't want to completely cut off their parents. So they "rappel" right out of the dilemma and into a world they aren't yet equipped to handle.

Jumping off a Cliff

Fourteen-year-old Daniel had always "performed" well in school. His parents had recently divorced, but Daniel appeared to be doing well. He and his dad connected primarily through performance-based activities—grades, sports, talking about Daniel's cute girlfriend. His mom, like most parents of adolescent boys, figured that as long as her son was getting good grades, mumbling a few sentences at the dinner table, and playing sports, he was doing great. But when Daniel began to act out at home and school and made some decisions that indicated he was headed to high-risk behavior, his mom sent him to counseling.

After six weeks of working together, I had come to know a boy who was sensitive in spirit, who was moved by close relationships, and who desired connection as much as — probably more than — all the achievements he could attain. The bummer for Daniel was that when things were going smoothly, everyone's focus was on the external. What was going on in his internal world was overlooked until he started getting into trouble. His grades had dropped from mostly As and Bs and a few Cs to a few Cs and mostly Ds. He was hanging out with the "wrong" crowd, drinking alcohol and experimenting with marijuana, and having angry outbursts at home.

When I do counseling with my clients, it always includes getting out of my office, with the goal of connecting in a creative way. Taking a teenager out for lunch or Frisbee golf or hiking alerts him to the fact that this relationship will be different from any therapeutic relationship he might have had before. He is more likely to start asking himself critical questions like, *Can I connect with this guy?* and *Is this the guy I should trust with my heart?*

I love rock climbing and mountaineering, and I've found that no other activity creates the opportunity to bond with my clients like these sports do. I'll never forget when I took Daniel rappelling down a sixty-five-foot overhanging rock cliff. I spent less than ten minutes covering safety tips and rope control and explaining how the equipment works. The crucial piece of equipment in the climbing and mountaineering world is the belay device, also known as the ATC. This is a two-inch-by-two-inch safety mechanism the main function of which is to apply enough pressure that if you pull the rope (literally with only one finger), you will stop—you will be safe. I told Daniel that he could use his belay device to stop his descent whenever it didn't feel safe, so that we could regroup and chart the next path down the rock face.

Without a single question or concern, Daniel took three big steps back to the overhang, and without hesitation he jumped off backward. He took a twenty-foot plunge. Although Daniel was fine and totally safe, I could not help but think of the wildness of this boy's heart and worry about where it might take him without any safety devices in place.

"How could you do that?" I asked Daniel. Before he answered, I knew. Daniel had been jumping out of the way for a long time. I recalled stories Daniel had told me of his jumping out of the way of his dad's anger and his mom's apathy toward his dad's aggressiveness. He had always felt like he was walking on eggshells with his dad. "In an attempt to connect, I would go into his home office almost every day to see how he was doing and see if he wanted to play catch, but I got thrown out regularly due to his work demands for the next day," he said. It was not uncommon for his dad to "discipline" Daniel with a smack on the back of the head for spilling milk or punish him with a weeklong silence for a more serious infraction. In the two years I worked with Daniel, his father participated in one session, during which he yelled at his son at the top of his voice about his poor performance with academics and sports (ironically he never participated with him but had huge expectations that Daniel would be a success). His antics freaked out some of the professionals who work upstairs, and the police were called to my office. Dad was escorted out. I had just a taste of what Daniel had been living with.

Soon before his parents divorced, Daniel had hidden his eighth-grade, second-semester report card for two days in fear of how his dad would react. When his dad did see the report card, he threw Daniel against the wall so hard that he went through the drywall. His dad's contemptuous accusation: "Obviously you didn't do a thing for the entire semester! What a loser!"

Daniel hated his dad's condemnation and angry outbursts. He had contempt for his mom, who became paralyzed during the heated conversations and abusive fighting. Many moms are like Daniel's — moms who are dealing with an angry father and a spirited son in a schizophrenic kind of way. They may do all the tasks of parenting well but then shut down completely when the fireworks between father and son begin.

I was concerned that Daniel's first rappel was a foreshadowing of his future. I suspected that Daniel would *search* for high-risk behaviors because of his personality type and because it was the only time he felt alive and the only place he felt safe. "Safe" in the midst of a sixty-five-foot free-fall rappel? Daniel trusted the two-inch-by-two-inch belay device to catch him, but he hadn't found that safety at home yet.

Grappling with Trust

Cody was another young man whose parents repelled him, which left him to figure out how to get down the mountain all by himself. Cody was sixteen years old when he went for his first rappel with me. When he was younger, he had been the kid who took risks, but as he grew into adolescence, something shifted and he became fear-based and anxious. After hearing some of the things his parents said to him (based on their own fears about all that could go wrong in the teen years), it wasn't hard to understand why Cody was so insecure. "Cody, you will be lucky if you ever get a girl to like you," his mom told him, "because to date you need money and a car and a place to go. You obviously have no place to go . . . look at what you're doing with yourself." Cody's parents discouraged his relationships with peers because "every adolescent boy uses drugs and is into pornography and lies to his parents." His mom repeatedly told her son that the only safe place on earth was home.

A few years of being told that the world is a scary place and you don't have what it takes to make it in that world made a huge difference in Cody. He adopted his parents' contagious anxiety. Rather than take risks, be shamed, and risk possible failure, Cody shut down. He withdrew from friends and family, showed signs of depression, and lacked enthusiasm for life.

I explained the rappel to Cody, and then, after I went through the same information I had with Daniel, it took Cody more than an hour before he would allow *me* to slowly lower him down the rock face. I was glad that Cody decided to trust me to help him, but I was saddened by his utter lack of trust in himself. Cody's insecurities put him through an agonizing hour on the edge of the cliff, grappling with trust. Since elementary school, Cody never felt that he had power. He felt as though everyone else were making the decisions for him. Now and then he tried bringing up a few ideas, questions, thoughts about himself and life. He would give it a shot and tell (usually) his mom something that he was thinking about, and mom would end up giving a moralistic lecture. Cody would see the hand in front of his face saying "Stop" and reach for his belay device at his hip, lowering himself out of the conversation, shutting down, and choosing not to participate.

At the end of both Daniel's and Cody's rappel, I was thrilled. Both boys had decided to take a risk, trust me, and accomplish something that would make them feel like they had some power in their lives. There's something about doing a task of heroic proportions—for Daniel, a backward leap off a cliff, and for Cody, a slow descent down a cliff tethered to a man whom he was beginning to trust—that can be life changing.

I have found that many teen boys crave a real person to relate to and to look to as a model for navigating the world. They usually don't find the appropriate model, who will hand them a rope, teach them about safety, give them tools to go for it, and then shout, "Jump!" Nevertheless, *they crave it.*

Connection and Safety

I observe one teen after another finding his own belay device—whether it's getting involved in music or sports, becoming a really good student, finding a girlfriend, or using drugs and alcohol. In response to his parent's posture of "Stop!" he grabs for the belay device at his hip, preparing to lower himself out of the situation.

At the beginning of this shift in relational dynamics, parent and teen want the same things. They want connection with each other and safety. But because connection and safety are defined differently by parents and teens, behaviors become entrenched pretty early that leave the parent with nothing more to say than, "Stop. Don't. Come back here," and the teenager with few options other than to get out of there. The result is that our natural, instinctive response to the challenges in preadolescence and adolescence is to send off signals to each other that will guarantee we won't get the things we want most—connection and safety in the context of an evolving and deepening relationship. And that is a major bummer. Kids are being overlooked, often when they need safety most. That's scary, because when a teen belays away from his parents, he is putting himself at risk to make stupid or even life-threatening decisions.

Kids are being missed in another way as well. Boys really want to share their hearts. Let me say that again. I am so tired of teenage boys being portrayed as one-dimensional, superficial, and nonrelational. Teenage boys want more than to be a jock, hook up with a girl, or drive a fast car. *They want to connect with another human being.*

If your son's behavior causes you to doubt this, just think about yourself for a moment. Maybe your job is going well, money is in the bank, and you get to play at a hobby or sport on the weekends. Everything's okay, right? But I imagine there are rumblings beneath the surface that tell you that you were made for more than being a performance machine. Teenage boys know this, so they act out—they do something stupid, foolish, or rebellious to say, "Stop looking at the outside—look at *me*!" A son's disturbing behavior can actually be very *good news*. Yes, good news! Because then we have an opportunity to look at him and our relationship with him from an entirely different angle.

When things appear to go off-kilter between parents and teenagers, fear and even disgust on both sides cause parents and teens to begin scrambling to get things back to homeostasis. Moms and dads generally want control and safety first; connection becomes a consolation prize. Most teens want connection first, and when that begins to seem unlikely as they notice that their questions and desires are not welcomed but shunned, a pattern of toxic reactions may develop. We're panicked that our sons' bad performances will result in bad boys, so we engage in interactions that sever connection. We talk at our kids instead of talking with them. We get frustrated at a behavior or a bad decision; it makes us feel uneasy or as though we're losing control, so we react instead of relate.

Contrary to what many parents believe, really *participating* in our kids' lives means we will feel uncomfortable and out of control on a regular basis! Bad performances may actually provide unprecedented *invitations* for us to really get to know our sons and connect with them, right in the midst of their struggles.

So how do you connect with a twelve- or sixteen-year-old boy when you're not twelve or sixteen? Of course, it's easier when our sons are compliant and self-motivated and enter into the challenges of adolescence with ease. But what about when they don't? Listen to the words of one of my fifteen-year-old clients, Jeremy: "Not many kids really want to be uncomfortable.

We will more times than not look for the easiest way out." Jeremy's honesty reminds us that we adults aren't that different from teenagers. When we're uncomfortable and uneasy, we find out what kind of parent we really are. If we look for the easy way out, not only might we lose our sons, but we might damage our own soul as well. We were created to connect in relationships. If we bail on the relationship with our son at the time he needs connection most, we're missing out on a big part of why we're on this earth.

Six Ways to Repel Your Son — Guaranteed

Toxic approaches to parenting usually occur because of a lack of education in parenting or of successful experiences in parenting your child so far. One father I worked with was reluctant to acknowledge that he didn't know what he was doing when it came to parenting, that he was making mistakes and causing some of the problems. This father is a heart surgeon. I asked him if he thought he could connect with my clients without being formally trained as a therapist. Likewise, I wondered if I could show up for an open-heart surgery and keep the patient alive with no formal training. He emphatically responded, "No." He got the point.

We as dads and moms need to approach parenting with humility and be able to acknowledge to ourselves, "This is not yet my strength." When we can truly humble ourselves, we're more likely to say, "This is not going well. I keep doing the same thing over and over and it is not effective. Who can I ask for help? Who can I turn to? Who would also truly have the best interests of my son's heart in mind?" I hope you can be in that posture as we examine six toxic approaches to interacting with teen boys—approaches that will certainly repel kids and ultimately push them away when they need us most.

Reacting

In reactionary communication there is one path to the conversation. It is often impulsive and immovable at the same time. A boy who is reacted to will either shut down or get out (which is the ultimate way of shutting down). For example, seventeen-year-old Jackson, star quarterback, is running off the field with his teammates after his school's first district championship win. He is pulled to the sideline by his father, who confronts him angrily about the fact that he threw one interception. "Dad," Jackson responds, "it was a bad play, but all my numbers were great and we won the game." His father loses it, yelling and screaming that his son should not even be allowed to be the quarterback because he can't make a wise decision under pressure. His son is crushed—not to mention mortified in front of his friends.

Parents who use reactionary communication will say things like, "What's wrong with you? Why are you doing this? Why can't you be like . . . ?" These questions/condemnations leave a teenager feeling like he has no choice but to get away (and usually act out) or to go inward to a locked world where no one will be able to ask questions he doesn't have answers for.

Micromanaging

Parents sensing that their son is entering a world of increasing chaos and opportunities for foolishness or danger may hyper-focus on one or two relatively insignificant areas for some sense of control. These parents become obsessed with their son keeping his room clean, listening to only Christian music, or getting good grades. They often overlook other, less tangible struggles, such as a decline in self-esteem or a withdrawal from peers, in order to focus on what seems more in their control. The end result is that either the teen will comply and do well in that one area but withdraw emotionally, or he will rebel completely and act out in several areas. Either way, there is disconnection.

I think the scarier disconnection is when teens comply and get great grades, while internally they become more and more depressed and draw destructive conclusions about who they are, whether others really care about them, or whether life is even worth living. All of this darkness and destruction is being hatched inside a teen while Mom and Dad think everything is great because homework is in on time and their son is on the honor roll. Hyperfocused, inflexible parents are often heard saying things like, "I don't care what you think. I'm the parent, and these are my rules."

Lecturing

Lecturing parents are unwilling to listen and unable to connect and truly hear their son. Sentences blend into one another, leaving our sons to hear us like the adults are "heard" on the Charlie Brown specials: "Wah-wah, wah-wah, wah-wah." Here's a challenge: Tell your son you have a feeling that you are lecturing rather than conversing. Ask him to give you a cue to let you know when he feels like a lecture is about to take off. It will take courage to stop in the moment and ask your son if there's anything *he'd* like to say. If yours is a home where lecturing is the primary mode of communication between parent and child, your son can very likely finish word-for-word any talk you begin. The problem isn't that he doesn't know what you believe and feel; it's that he can't connect your beliefs and feelings to his. The result is severed connection.

Moralizing

Moralizing often takes place in a home where a teenage boy comes home with Ds and Fs on his report card. Nik was that boy. Both of his parents were highly educated and were shocked by Nik's academic performance. His mom would start down the path of moralizing after looking at the report card: "Don't you understand that this impacts your future. . . . I mean, it could impact your job, where you live, the kind of girl who wants to marry you. . . ." She wouldn't stop, and she continued to use this one report card to "horriblize" every part of Nik's future life. It's no wonder to me that this kid didn't want to do any schoolwork. One wrong turn could doom his whole life!

Moralizing feeds our kids the law, and they choke on it. They realize that even if they could do it all perfectly, it wouldn't be enough. There's always another thing to do. When performance is tied to identity, kids in moralistic homes live either with a sense of drivenness ("I must perform to be a good person") or a sense of despair ("I can't do it well enough, so *I* must be bad"). Moralistic parents say things like, "Don't you realize that this is getting you nowhere good, fast? I can't believe what a loser/idiot/waste of space you are." All these abusive sentiments translate into "You'll amount to nothing."

Reiterating

In some families, parents say the same things over and over again. Many parents suggest that they *have* to do this because things aren't changing. They believe it's the child's fault for doing the same things over and over. Usually not. Parents say the same things over and over because those are the things that they know. They may try to change things up, but teenagers are experts at identifying agendas; rather than join our agenda, they'll grab their belay and shut up, withdraw, shut down, and get away from home (usually emotionally first) as fast as possible. Signs of repetition include beginning sentences with, "I know I've said this before . . ." or "How many times do I have to tell you?"

I feel your frustration mounting: "Well, if he'd just do the right thing, I wouldn't have to be a nag." I have good news and bad news. *It doesn't matter how many times you say it.* Unless there's *connection* between you and your son, *he can't hear you.* We will be focusing in this book on forging the link that will enable him to actually hear you and you to hear him. Only from this improved connection will true change flow. It might not be the exact change you want, but you will be okay with that as you grow to understand that what you really want is a relationship and not robotic compliance with your requests.

Threatening

The parent who uses absolutes and ultimatums delivers threats that can't be lived up to or enforced. "You're not going out again until you graduate!" Why would parents make such a ridiculous statement? Because they feel threatened and believe that by threatening the worst, they will be able to get their son to fall into line. It seldom works that way. The parent looks like a fool. When a parent throws out threats and the kid says, "Whatever," I know there is a long history of idle threats.

Ultimatums imprison parents and enrage teenagers. Yes, it really makes them mad to be threatened and then have the threat disregarded. A teen feels like you are playing with him. Often when teens go out, they are sent off with a threat. "If you don't call me when you get there, I'm going to find you and bring you home. You'll be sorry." For boys, a threat of retribution hanging over their head will inspire them to match out in their world what has been presented to them at home, murmuring under their breath, "*You'll* be sorry."

The 90-Second Window

Perhaps you find yourself stuck in a reactionary, hyperfocused, lecturing, moralizing, repetitive, or threatening pattern of communication. It's difficult to change the momentum of communication, but it's not impossible. I have found a strategy that helps moms and dads step out of unhealthy modes of communication and step toward communication that might actually open the door to meaningful connection with their sons.

Here's a fact you probably don't want to know, but listen up: You have only about *ninety seconds* to connect with your son in a specific conversation. For the first thirty seconds your son is attempting to figure out, "Have I heard this before? What are they trying to get me to do?" Kids are usually willing to listen for the first thirty seconds.

During the second thirty seconds teens are trying to place themselves within the information. They may be asking, "Where can I agree with Mom? Is this something new? Is this positive, negative, doable?"

The last thirty seconds is the kid's way out. He thinks, *I've heard this. I understand this.* He's reaching for his belay: *Okay, this is my action plan. This is how I get out of here.* Teenage boys think linearly, not globally. They think to themselves, *I have this piece of information, I have heard how this information is impacting my mom and how it impacts me,* which translates into, *Where do I go from here? How do I assimilate Mom's information into my world with the least amount of work?*

Now before you get defensive and say, "It shouldn't be that way. They should listen and respond. That's why this is the lost generation," take a few minutes and really try to get it here. We parents are responsible for teaching communication skills to our kids. Withdrawal or shutting down is a pattern that teens use to their advantage, and it feels like a skill because it enables them to get what they want. We know it's not a skill. It's a detriment, the result of which is disconnection, and it's our job to help them understand that. If we don't, ultimately, we won't even get thirty seconds.

Let me suggest that you start with a commitment to be brief

in your interactions with your son. You might begin with, "I want to talk to you about one thing (be upbeat). Just give me ninety seconds." Your son will perk up. *This is new*, he might think. He is open. Then keep your agreement and back it up with something tangible. Tell him that if you go over time, he gets five dollars. Express concern about one thing: "I'm worried about your D- in math." Your first thirty seconds is gone. Your son is wondering, *What's going to happen; what does she want from me?* Ask him, "What are you willing to do to take care of that grade?" If he doesn't have an immediate answer, ask him to get back to you when he has one idea of what he might do. Your second thirty seconds is gone. Smile and say, "I'm sure you can think of something. Gotta go." Your third thirty seconds is gone, hopefully before he has checked out. You've left him wondering what is up with you, and you've planted a seed: "I believe in you. You can take care of this." Ninety seconds and you've given your son one of the most important messages of growing up: "You need to take responsibility. I am here to help. I believe you can do it."

If talking directly with your son proves to be too great of a challenge for either of you — even for ninety seconds — don't give up. Try writing out no more than three thoughts on a note card. Be clear, concise, and constructive. Write out the problem. Ask for something. Share an observation or feeling. Hand your son the card and say, "I want to see how you're going to handle this." Guys need tactile objects, something to hold onto. The card can be a powerful tool if your heart for your son is positively portrayed on it.

Here's an example of a card one parent used:

1. Your little brother is not getting picked up after school.
2. Can you pick him up every day or call me before noon, to let me know that you can't?
3. I think this will work because I know you care about your brother and don't want him feeling afraid and confused when you don't show up.

The 90-second strategy is about giving your son a chance to make a choice. He can face the choice and make a good decision or take the consequence. Thousands of interactions like this (ninety seconds at a time) will make a difference. Yes, thousands. For every month one of my guys has spent developing bad skills, it takes me twice as long to undo the negative relational consequences that have accumulated. That's two months of weekly sessions, eight hours in his world, trying to develop a positive relationship and give him a sense that he is really being heard. My question for you is, How will you find and use eight hours in your teen's life over the next two months?

Turning Weakness to Strength

I'm often asked by parents, youth pastors, and counselors, "Which parent does the average youth complain more about?" Without exception my guys complain more about their moms, because they are in the habit of compensating for their fathers. Did you hear that, moms? They are complaining about you — not because it is all your fault, but because they've been conditioned to let their dads off the hook. One of the reasons boys pardon their dads is because they feel sorry for them. They are tired of their moms complaining about Dad's poor parenting and communication skills. And boys quickly become overwhelmed and exhausted by moms who use every minute of those eight hours to compensate for Dad, saying twice as much, showing up twice as often, and struggling to make up for the fact that dads aren't usually educated in connecting because the modeling they received as a child, in general, was, "Suck it up, and be a man."

Here's my suggestion for you, Mom. Put less emphasis on vocabulary. Slow things down. Don't give quite so much information. Be present. Use the adage, "Check yourself before you wreck yourself." Are *any* of the comments you make meant to point out Dad's deficiencies? Cut it out. Asking your son to join you in anger and frustration about his dad will backfire big time. Your son will be confused about being a man and angry at women who keep telling him to show up and automatically know what's expected of him.

As a mom or dad it's not easy to hear that we are actually *repelling* our children. Acknowledging our weakness or inability to connect with our son allows us to disclose our own deficiencies, seek help from others, take suggestions, and grow with our son rather than be out in front of him, warning him to "Stop!" or yelling at him to "Suck it up!" When we can get to this humble place of true strength (over and over and over again), then *the chase is on.*

GO FOR IT!

ON YOUR MARKS!

Ask your son when you can have ninety seconds of his time. That shows your willingness to make an effort. If he blows you off and doesn't get back to you, approach him again and in the fewest possible sentences communicate, "I am trying to do something different. There is one thing I need to talk to you about. I promise it will look different. Are you willing to give it a shot?" Even hearing that, your son's heart will become more sensitive to hearing what you have to say. If that doesn't work, tell your son that he needs to give you ninety seconds or you're going to shave his head in his sleep — that usually gets a young man's attention!

GET SET!

Ask for what you want from your son. When a parent does not communicate a clear expectation, it leads to anger and frustration. In other words, be direct. "What are you willing to do about your grade in geometry?" or "Can we agree on a midnight curfew with immediate, short-term consequences for blatantly dishonoring this expectation?" Some necessary joint problem solving is involved in this kind of communication, and that fosters *connection*.

GO!

Whenever you present your son with a problem to solve, tell him you are looking forward to seeing how he will remedy the situation and you will make yourself available to help him problem-solve. End your conversation with "What do you think?" and wait for a response. If he says he doesn't know, remind him that "I don't know" is not an answer. Stick around and see where he takes you in the conversation. As you wait patiently and ask different questions, you're more likely to see him coming back to you rather than rappelling out of the relationship.

3

Weathering the Storms

Recall the story from the beginning of chapter 1, in which our group was stranded in the middle of a storm on Longs Peak? You may be in the middle of a storm yourself. A storm in which the visibility is nil, and you can't see what the next step toward safety might be. You don't know when there might be a break in the weather, if the storm will get worse, or if it will ever end at all.

Storms come from so many different directions, and parents who aren't paying attention — I mean *really* paying attention — may not be aware of what their actions and words are saying to their sons about the storm. When I paid attention to our surroundings during our mountaineering experience and yelled for everyone to get ready for another storm, you can believe the guys hung on every word. They knew I was not naive about storms, and they wanted a guide they could trust. Boys want their parents to be trustworthy guides when adolescent storms are raging, but parents tend to react in ways that virtually guarantee their son won't "hang on their every word" when the storm blows in.

For example, parents tend to say things like, "We don't yell in this family" or "You don't talk to me like that." When our son walks in the door after having a bad day and acts like a "punk" or is aggressive, we mirror his behavior rather than asking questions or waiting for his mood to settle. When we say things like, "Get out of this house and come back when you've mellowed out," we are letting our son know that his home is not his haven from the storm. It doesn't feel good to be the target of an adolescent boy's hostility, but when we preach or scold, we let him know that we are not the guide he's looking for.

Parents often don't handle stress any better than their kids. After all, we have a lot on our plates. There are bills to pay, our marriages need attention, and we're not exactly sure what we're doing in the whole parenting department. We have our own storms, which might keep us from talking to each other in meaningful ways about our boys. We don't ask questions; we blame each other, assume the worst, or ignore the problem altogether.

One of my clients was caught by an older cousin looking at porn in his father's bedroom. He was paraded before his parents while his cousin held up the magazine and mocked, "Look what this little loser is doing." The thirteen-year-old's dad ripped the magazine from his hands, and there was never any further conversation about the event. The shame and contempt haunted him for years and led him into further exploration of a secret world he didn't understand. The storm of a pornography addiction began with silence.

Brett is another good example of what can happen when parents aren't anticipating or prepared for storms. Brett was sixteen when he came to see me. He had lost his driver's license for too many speeding tickets, so Mom was responsible for driving him to school. Her resentment brewed as Brett's anger continued to boil unaddressed. He didn't share a lot of personal information with either parent. One day when Mom picked Brett up from school, he got into the car, slammed the door, and started ranting and raving (using the "F" word many times) because he was angry about teachers, classmates, not having a car, and so much more.

Following this great after-school moment, his mom came to my office looking harried and disheveled—like she'd been through a storm. "He said the 'F' word at least *eleven* times! I can't believe it!" She began to react.

I stopped her. "Tell me what *else* you heard him say."

"Well . . ." Mom thought for a minute. "He told me about his teacher, peers. . . . Wait," she suddenly realized, "Brett was talking about his *life*. He hasn't talked to me about much of anything for a long time."

This mom was beginning to understand how to weather a storm. Is the issue that Brett said the "F" word eleven times or that he was *telling stories* (or at least the headlines to his stories) for the first time in a long time? If we react rather than relate, then we will be ineffective when the storms of adolescence (minor or extreme) hit.

Hang Back and Show Up

Kids live to talk about what is going on in their lives—externally and internally. For boys, their message is, "Please, help me win. Help me figure out how to navigate this world I'm in and not be a loser, a failure, alone." Boys, however (like a lot of men), aren't good at asking for help. They will keep to themselves and process for hours ways they can be in charge and manipulate their parents. I tell parents that kids, on average, will spend six to eight hours every day thinking about that process: simply, *How can I get what I want?* It may be healthy processing. I have a friend whose son would spend hours on the computer looking up jobs, qualifications for the jobs, and salaries. He was only fifteen, but he was trying to figure out how to win. Or the processing may be destructive, even to the point of colluding with peers in order to get the desired result—"My mom's never going to let me go out this weekend unless I come up with some plan. . . ." Parents, on the other hand, will generally spend less than ten minutes a day thinking about how they can connect with their son regarding his passionate desire to "win." When your son is spending six to eight hours alone or with peers planning his life, and you're thinking about it (in terms of how he can be successful and feel like a winner) for ten minutes a day, you're *not* prepared to weather any storms with him.

I realize that not every parent spends only ten minutes a day thinking about their child's success. Some parents are on the opposite end of the continuum and that's *all* they think about. I caution you to evaluate whether you are thinking about your agenda for your son or how you can help him understand his own agenda and act on it in a way that increases his sense of identity and positive independence.

Thomas is a good example of a young man whose family was in the middle of a storm—but totally unprepared. At sixteen, Thomas was a daily pot smoker and a binge drinker. Neither of his parents had a clue as to what was truly going on with him. This is not to say that either parent was a bad parent. They were just not keeping up with what was happening inside their son, much less how he was coping with it. They were busy with *their* jobs, friends, and hobbies. Meanwhile, Thomas and some of his friends had created their own little society, lacking any meaningful adult involvement. Author Patricia Hersh describes what often happens in teenagers' lives where parents are too busy focusing on their own lives: "They [kids] have been forced by a personal sense of abandonment to band together and create their own world—separate, semi-secret, and vastly different from the world around them."[1]

Ron Taffel, author of *The Second Family*, says that the average teenager engages in eight minutes of meaningful conversation with an adult each day.[2] That leaves kids understimulated by healthy, constructive influences, while at the same time being overstimulated by cultural pressures (particularly by media). Or the family may be focused on survival, so there's no tangible anticipation for the future. There is nothing more depressing—and just plain *boring*—to a teenager than being without a vision for personal success and relational connection.

One of my clients wrote a poem that poignantly describes his sense of aimlessness at the age of only fifteen.

WHY?

Why do we live to die?
I just want the reason why
To feel the emotion bottle up
To watch this world become more corrupt
Why do we live to die?

Why don't we have any power?
To watch life pass and wither like a dying flower
To find the world's true writhe and heart
To have a life that is broken apart
Why don't we have any power?

Why is there so much pain?
Is there no other way to remove the stain?
To watch life cycle through
To have pain through and through
Why is there so much pain?

Why do we try?
The point is just to live to die
The feeling is full of hate
Isn't this world great?
Why do we try?

The truth is, many teenagers are bored out of their minds and emotionally flattened (or inflamed) by a sense of futility. The result can be a disconnect from a cognitive moral sense of right and wrong, leading to a choice to meet their needs in the moment with alcohol, drugs, sex, aggression, etc. These, of course, are temporary highs; then there is a letdown, greater boredom, and an even fiercer determination to start the process all over again. *Boredom is often the symptom of an extreme storm about to hit.* Boys are naturally assertive and adventurous. When they are bored, they will try to find things to do, and sadly, they often choose destructive or extreme behaviors, further distancing them from what they want most: true connections with friends and family.

If we want to have relational breakthroughs with our adolescent sons, we need to understand what they are really aiming for with their strategies — no matter how bizarre those strategies may appear to us. More than anything else, *teenage boys are telling a story.* Their story. They desperately want someone — ideally, their own parents — to hear them.

Shoulder-to-Shoulder Communication

Thomas made plenty of bad choices in his attempts to anesthetize his feeling of personal disconnection at home. After school one day he pulled out an old BB gun and pointed it at a female student driving next to him. He was arrested for felony menacing and held on $50,000 bail. His parents couldn't bail him out until the next day. He had to get drug tested, which yielded a positive result for marijuana. The storm hit, and all of a sudden his parents found out a lot about their son. They said to me, "We thought he was such a good kid. We thought everything was going so well with him."

Thank goodness Thomas steered his parents right into a big pothole, and everything from the back of the car came flying into the front seat. They could no longer deny what was really there. They tried to put restrictions on Thomas, but they were about four years behind in their storm preparation. They tried to create a system of rules, but Thomas had been doing his own thing for too long. He would not keep the rules, and his acting out resulted in one catastrophic event after another. Thomas would break curfew, drink to excess, and lie about his whereabouts. Eventually, his parents made the hard decision to send their son to a treatment center for alcohol and drug abuse.

Our children's pain and problems either force us to confront reality and make changes or drive us further away from the chaos of the storm. Thomas's parents chose to find out what made their son tick and what messages they had missed before the storm hit full force. Their "education" began with the eighteen-hour car ride to drive their decidedly unhappy son to treatment. I explained to them that this could be the worst car ride they would ever experience, or it could be an opportunity for them to hear — *really* hear — Thomas's story. This would no doubt require that they hang back — that is, create an environment that felt safe enough to Thomas that he would do what he most wanted to do deep down inside: talk about his life — but also be ready to show up. They employed a strategy that I'd seen work countless times in my own interactions with teenagers. Rather than get in their son's face, rather than pummel him with questions or demands for explanation, they wisely and patiently waited for Thomas to come to them.

This happens most naturally when parents and teens are

already shoulder to shoulder, doing something, maybe something the parents are not even interested in. This could be listening to your son's music, hanging out together in stores he likes, going fishing, watching a movie together, or taking a drive. If your kid invites you to do something, you *need* to respond and accept the invitation. Even if you find something objectionable in your son's interests, don't flat-out refuse. Look for something good first. Find out why your son is interested in this. Then use it to make a connection, shoulder to shoulder.

One of my wife's good friends is a dog lover and was visiting a family who had a golden retriever. Upon greeting them, the dog's family explained to my wife's friend that the retriever wanted to give her a kiss. Making direct eye contact with the friendly golden, she bent over to pet him. He jumped up and bit her in the face, tearing off part of her lip.

Adolescents may look like golden retrievers (or pit bulls), but what I've found is that face-to-face contact is intimidating for them. They don't know how to express themselves easily and effortlessly, so if someone stands opposite them and pleads for communication, they often respond with a bite. And being bitten by a hostile teen hurts! Do they mean to terrorize us? No! But they are experts at inducing panic. Remember, what they are actually looking for is success in relationships. They are looking for someone to join them and walk alongside them. Some of my best connections with kids come when they are sitting diagonal from me or walking next to me or doing some activity *with* me.

First-time clients will often sit across from me because that is the assumed position in therapy, but they are almost always uncomfortable. Therapists are usually trained to work face-to-face with their clients, but this rarely works with teen-age boys. So pretty quickly, we'll get out of the office and find a context in which we can be side by side. This becomes the posture that allows communication to begin. After a few sessions with me, when we do stay in the office, guys will sit diagonally from me (two to three feet away), because this is how they most naturally connect.

Moms, you know this is true whether you realize it or not. You generally do the best connecting with your son because you are spending the most time *next* to him — riding in the car, doing geography homework, or sitting on the back porch throwing a ball for your dog. I have a friend who told me that when her son started to drive himself to school, he would occa-sionally ask her if she could drive him. When she asked, "Why in the world do you want me to take you to school when you can finally drive yourself?" he replied, "I just miss our drives." He was missing that shoulder-to-shoulder connection.

Some of you will find it counterintuitive to sit alongside your son or choose activities with him that put you shoul-der to shoulder, and then *let* the conversation unfold rather than steering it. But I know too many stories about boys who have self-destructed because their parents would not make a simple change in the posture of their communication — from face-to-face, to shoulder to shoulder. I have a friend who has had great conversations with his son while sitting next to him in a movie theater waiting for a movie to begin. He purposely makes sure they arrive early so there will be a little time for conversation. The mother of one client goes skeet shooting with her son. She never hits a single target, but there are good conversations in the car on the way to and from the shooting range and between shooting times.

Well, Thomas's parents were in for some good conversation on that eighteen-hour car ride. Thomas eventually told his mom and dad the entire story of his drug and alcohol use, and a whole lot of things that went along with it. His parents listened, got mad, got sad, but ultimately got into their son's world.

During a particularly intense point in the conversation, Thomas's mom learned an invaluable lesson — straight from the mouth of her son. "Mom, this isn't about you. This is about me, making some bad decisions." His mom told me later that when she finally understood that her son's choices were not a reflection of who *she* was, she was more ready than ever to listen to *his* story. "Learning to separate myself from what he was doing was so hard," she said. "That long car ride was a very healing time for us. Thomas gave us the gift of honesty. He continues to tell us stories of things he and his buddies did, now as a way of healing."

Some months after Thomas came home from treatment, his courageous dad wrote to me, "I am thankful for the probing in my life that caused some self-evaluation and changes that I hope will make me a better father and husband." As Thomas's parents began to realize that they could handle their son's honest disclosures without going ballistic, they also began to believe that they really could be effective guides through the storms that would surely come again.

Trying Something New

By the time I see adolescent boys in my counseling office, they are often drowning in self-hatred, depression, isolation, and secretive behaviors. Life starts to feel desperate. That's why teens bite.

Many parents feel outgunned by their son's energy when it's negative, and most are overwhelmed and uninformed. Many feel hopeless; some are just trying to catch up; and few have the skills and support to strategically guide their son through some pretty rough storms of adolescence. The stakes are high and the pressure is on. Let me bottom-line three strategies for you that will increase your likelihood of weathering the storms of the teen years.

PURSUE RATHER THAN HUNT. Your son comes home and you ask, "How was your day?" "Fine," he grunts. "I don't want to talk about it." And then he goes downstairs. You hunt him down, "*Please* tell me what's going on." You just want to engage. Then he yells, "Get out of my room!" You continue to hunt. It's now about your need to connect rather than his need to be left alone, process, and come to you when he's ready to talk. Sometimes parents *need* to know what's happening with their sons because they are making it more about themselves than their boys.

Parents also try to wear camouflage gear and sneak around and "spy" on their kids by asking seemingly innocent questions that have hidden meaning, such as, "Is that one friend who got in trouble at school going to be at this party?" Teenagers are experts at sniffing you right out of your hiding place. Pursuing is being able to admit, "I don't know how to have a good, growing relationship with you, but I want one. I want to finish the last years before you go to college with a closer relationship." *Ask* how you can have a relationship with them. And then give them some time and space to respond. They'll show you.

BE FLEXIBLE AND CREATIVE. Here are just a couple of ways parents I've known have chosen to show up. At my suggestion one dad went to his son's school fifteen minutes before lunchtime and asked the attendance counselor to get his son so he could take him out to lunch. When the son heard his dad was at school, he was freaked out, thinking that something was wrong or that he was in big trouble. When he found out that his dad was only there to be with him and that they were just going to have some time together over lunch, he was blown away—and even more so when Dad suggested they blow off the entire afternoon and go to a movie together. The dad told me later how nervous he was when he walked into the school and when he saw his son approaching him. He was unsure of what they would talk about since he usually stuck to asking his "top five questions" (how was school, how was that paper or test, how is your girlfriend, etc.). He found that by letting his son take the lead, he heard more information over that lunch hour than he had in the previous four years. Dad was overjoyed and amazed at how well it went, especially when his son asked if they could "do this every week." They now have a designated time once a week that is just for them. They go to movies, have dinner, go on hikes, or do community service together. The relationship has improved immeasurably from where they were. The son now text-messages his dad, and vice versa, just to stay in touch when they're apart.

When the son of a friend wanted to get a tattoo, rather than freak out, she asked her son to research it. She acted like she didn't know everything (which she didn't) or maybe anything—at least not about tattoos. Her son found out about the history of tattoos and discovered the symbology (especially religious) behind many tattoos. His mom found herself thinking some of those tattoos would be pretty cool. In response to her interest in his interest, her son lost interest (for the time being) in getting a tattoo. A couple of years later he did pick a tattoo, and his mom asked me to go with him when he had it done. Mom didn't think she could actually *watch* the procedure, but she could be supportive because she had intentionally changed her parenting style.

PERSEVERE. This all sounds easy on paper, doesn't it? But hanging in there and being patient *is* the job of parenting. Most of us are too impatient. We won't wait because it gets frustrating. We have this 160-pound statue in front of us, and we can't make him move.

I work with a lot of guys who are quiet. I have to force myself to shut up and wait. In graduate school I learned that I should not ask "closed" questions like, "How was your day?" because the response might be a meaningless "Fine." My own model of counseling challenges that graduate school advice. I have learned that even the tone of the "Fine" can give me a peek at what is going on inside.

Thomas's parents sat through an eighteen-hour car ride to wait and listen for their son's story to come out. And eventually it did. And it's still coming. Thomas's mom sometimes calls me when she starts freaking out because Thomas's attitude is bad or because he is sullen or withdrawn and simply saying "Fine" in a way that means anything but "Fine." When I remind her that pursuing a boy *while* freaking out will guarantee that he won't want to share information, it usually doesn't take her long to regain her bearings and get back to the wise strategy of hanging back and showing up. "Thomas still struggles to do the right thing," she told me recently, "but the good news is that he is struggling and thinking and talking about it."

Albert Einstein said that insanity is "doing the same thing over and over again and expecting different results." Parents are insane when they try the same relational skills over and over and expect their son to all of a sudden show up and engage. True connection grows out of continuity and consistency. I coach parents on showing up and standing in the gap for their sons on a daily basis. Young men are so eager to know their parents will invest time in them and for them that time with or around them can often soften their spirit.

Remember, your son is a story in progress. Let his story unfold as he is *with* you — not in front of you or behind you. If you don't want to feel nuts, then try something new. Hang back a little. Give him a chance to show up, and be ready to do the same. Then *the chase is on.*

GO FOR IT!

ON YOUR MARKS!

Say to your son, "I want to know the top three things you're interested in. I want to get educated about them and see where we can go with them." You might feel uncomfortable with some of your son's interests, but he will feel like you care about him. And if you feel uncomfortable, then you are definitely "going for it"!

GET SET!

If your son does tell you a story, don't give him a blank stare and try not to go ballistic. Take a break if you need to—use any excuse to separate if you think you will blow it—but then come back and tell him how huge it was to hear his heart. That will encourage him to offer you more.

GO!

Focus on listening first rather than debating or criticizing or telling your son to do it "this way." Keep asking him questions, but don't go crazy if he shuts down. Communicate to him that you are trying something new and you want his input on how he thinks this is going, then listen to anything he has to say and try to apply it to your next interaction. Trying to communicate with someone you have not really communicated with in a long time will take dedication. Keep your impatience in check, and keep going for it.

4

Breaking the Rules

My heart is huge for the boys who come to my office full of undirected and uncared-for energy and passion. I was that boy. It's not hard for me to recall the shame of not knowing what to do with myself, the embarrassment of disappointing my parents, and then the hardened rebellion of not caring if I kept myself in check. I really just wanted someone to pay attention, see me for who I was, and *meet me there.*

How does it feel to you in relationships when you are overlooked or dismissed for who you are? Teenagers are no different from us. They are human too. Not long ago I was with one of my clients, and we were eating some pretty spicy burritos. I noticed that his drink was almost empty, so when the waitress came and asked how we were doing I ignored the eighteen-year-old's "Fine, thanks." I have four children, all under the age of seven, so I instinctively interjected: "I think his drink is getting a little low. He might want a refill." My client glared at me. When I said, "What's up?" he answered angrily, "If I want another drink, I can ask for one."

He was telling me he no longer needs to be parented like a seven-year-old. This encounter with a client reminded me of how much more difficult it is for parents dealing with their own children to make the leap from the rules of childhood to a whole new set of ever-evolving rules during adolescence. I know all too well from my counseling practice that when parents don't make the leap, both teen and parent often end up falling into a chasm of disconnection and destruction. My collision with my client over a simple soft drink reminded me that making this leap takes courage and perception.

Parents who are terrified, ill-equipped, or undereducated may hope that it will all go away—their son's growing independence, adventurous energy, aggression, and anger that no one is "getting" him—so they ignore it, feel intimidated, feel uncomfortable, or just get more rigid. They don't know what to do, except to do what feels most familiar, which is to play by the old rules. Many parents, especially dads, are embarrassed to admit that things aren't working and fear that asking for help will reveal *their* failure and make them look weak.

I could have matched my client's contempt for me over ordering the soft drink with contempt for him by saying, "Man, I was just trying to be nice. Not to worry, I won't go out of my way for you again!" It is dismaying to me how often we match a teen's angry, disrespectful behavior with the same behavior. Instead I said, "My bad. I'm used to eating with my own small children. *I forgot who you are.*"

When we parent in an outmoded style or by old rules, we are telling our children, "I can't see you. I forget who you are." Our weaknesses or comfort zones in parenting compel us to stay stuck in tracks that undervalue our sons. The face-to-face style discussed in the previous chapter, for example, is often a reflection of our reluctance to educate ourselves about our need to evolve as parents and may reveal our lack of sensitivity to what our son is comfortable with and what will ultimately connect us to him.

A good example of how boys change in the ways they communicate can be easily observed in the hallways of your son's middle school or high school. Information is chattered among kids as they walk through the halls. Kids moving into adolescence are learning that this is the way to do it. Communicating face-to-face — even with peers they are close to — is intimidating. It undermines the system that is working socially. Parents who continue to parent their fourteen-year-old the same ways they parented their ten-year-old will get into a communication power struggle that their teenager will always win.

"He Was Such a Sweet Little Boy . . ."

This chapter may be challenging for some of you who have believed that consistent rule keeping is the key to successful parenting. I have found that consistent rule keeping consistently results in rebellion, power struggles, and disconnection between teenager and parent. Breaking the rules is important in parenting because it keeps your child guessing what may come next.

By age three our kids know which parent they can manipulate. By age five they are really clear on rules and understand breaking them and the potential consequences or lack of consequences in the family system. They're clear on what a lie is and what truth is. By age six they can already see that we, as their parents, are predictable in our patterns of reacting, disciplining, and encouraging. Our frustrations and joys are plain to see.

With children who are already familiar with the ins and outs of the rule keeping in the family, it's essential to understand that if we play by the same set of rules consistently for eighteen years of parenting, our children will tire of our system or become angry. When we use the same rules or manner of expressing our values to our sixteen-year-old as we did to our six-year-old, our sons will put us in a box: "My parents think I'm a child. They don't understand. I can't trust them. I need to find a way to get around them." When our sixteen-year-old starts "getting around us" and breaking the rules, we are tempted to put him in a box and make the rules even more numerous or more rigid. I can't tell you how many parents have expressed to me with despair, "He was such a sweet little boy. I don't know what happened."

What happened is that he is no longer a little boy. He grew a brain, and every cell in his body yearns for the normal developmental tasks of adolescence, such as independence and identity-development. Remember when you were sixteen and craved being free for just a moment, so you asked to run to the grocery store with the family car and stopped along the way to hang out at a friend's house? Kids have not changed. Teens long for independence and for flexibility regarding the rules and expectations from their childhood.

However, the adolescent population and environment *have*

changed. Sex saturates the teen world, drugs are more available, much of the music is offensive, and anger is more prominently worn on the sleeve of every teen boy. I understand that the idea of easing up on the old rules seems scary. Parents are reluctant to meet kids where they are and consider changes. We foolishly want kids to meet us where we are. That will result in consistent disappointment on our part, pretense on our kids' part (like the Eddie Haskell syndrome from the old *Leave It to Beaver* television series), or anger at our failure to recognize where they are. We cannot ask our teens to play by Candy Land rules when they have graduated to far more complex and difficult games.

When we try to enforce old rules or even implement new, more appropriate rules, a teenager may respond with an upright hand in our faces. It's easy for our egos to get in the way of our ability to look around the hand when it's directly in front of our face. The hand says, "I don't need you or want you to participate in this part of my world." Teens put up this big hand as if to say, "You're coming at me too fast, with too much — I can order my own soft drink!" But believe it or not, they are still peering (ever so covertly) around that hand, saying to us, "Please hang in there with me."

Teens have their own set of rules among themselves. They have their own society, and often parents are not invited in. You break the rules when you acknowledge you blew it, you missed something good, misunderstood something troubling—you forgot who they were or didn't recognize what they were dealing with. Breaking the rules allows you to be a little more present in your teen's real world. It gives you permission to show up and participate instead of scrambling for the "right" thing to do to guarantee that a certain behavior is nipped in the bud. When you allow only the rule book to be your guide, your kid will either look good on the outside while simmering inside with anger, hurt, and resentment, or the toxicity will ooze out of his pores as he acts out all over the place.

I'm not suggesting that you throw out all the rules and just see what happens. Breaking the rules can lead to chaos, so you must be prepared. A change of approach in your parenting will not work if you are not structured in your new tack. You'll end up with your kids climbing the walls or climbing out windows if you aren't considering rule breaking as part of a larger strategy to connect.

Breaking the rules will surprise your kids, and they'll be watching to see if this is a one-time deal or if you are really noticing their changing world and trying to adapt in a way that keeps them safe but makes them feel respected. Later in this chapter I will give you some specific examples of how to break the rules while maintaining a safe and stable environment for your family.

Teenagers Are Like Crock-Pots

The consistent theme I hear in my office is that kids feel trapped in a bubble of performance and expectations, some spoken and some unspoken. Kids are human Crock-Pots. They throw into the pot their conflict with Mom and Dad over being grounded, their relationship issues at home and at school, peer conflicts and expectations, and they are on low simmer (or higher) every day.

Over time the heat dries up any fluid, and the Crock-Pot will crack and even explode if it's not turned off and cleaned out.

More often than not this is what happens during adolescent disconnection. A son runs away from home because his parents are "all over him" for not cleaning his room. A boy withdraws into a dark world of video games and chat rooms because he believes his parents will only chastise him for anything he expresses. A kid turns to drugs or sexual acting out because it makes him feel more alive than languishing in a boring family dynamic that's fixated on the rules of his childhood.

Following the old rules can be a hindrance to positive change. If we can proactively upset the family rules, we will empower ourselves. A therapist friend of mine told me the story of one family that had rules set in concrete. It was a homeschool family that was all of a sudden facing a son who was sneaking out, smoking cigarettes, and wanting nothing to do with the family. Mom kept trying to rein him in with the old rules, but this fifteen-year-old was done with the rules of childhood. The old system just made him run and hide. When his mom saw that hunting down her son and aiming a shotgun full of rules was not only accomplishing nothing, but was destroying their relationship entirely, she sought counseling.

After a period of counseling that enabled her to see her part in her son's rebellion, she got the concept that rules minus relationship almost always equals rebellion in teenagers. She and her husband got on the same page and decided to break some rules in a tangible way. One Saturday morning after breakfast Dad told all three of their sons, aged eleven to fifteen, to take their ceramic cereal bowls out to the concrete patio. He led the way by smashing his bowl to smithereens and invited the rest of the family to do likewise. He explained, "We need to change some rules around here to reflect your growing up and changing lives. Let's smash some dishes!" As they stood in the ruins of their cereal bowls, the eleven-year-old, with eyes as wide as dinner plates, exclaimed, "Is this for real?"

This bowl-smashing episode was a first step for these parents toward capturing the attention and heart of their sons, especially their fifteen-year-old's. In his attempt to connect and have relationships, their oldest son had been making some bad choices, like smoking and disengaging from his family. His parents were generally stringent about the rules, no matter the cost to their kids. In the wake of their oldest child's acting out, they became willing to loosen their parenting paradigm in order to change the relational dynamic and pursue their son's heart in new ways. "Having it all together" as a family became less important than connecting. In the process of playing by a revised rulebook, this son shared a lot of information with both parents, and the anger slowly dissipated as the Crock-Pot of emotion was cleaned out rather than sealed up.

When Breaking the Rules Means Backing Off

When we are willing to stir things up in our families and notice that change is necessary because our children are changing, we capture the attention of our sons.

I worked with one dad who came in totally frustrated. His

sixteen-year-old stepson had always been such a good boy. He was respectful, helpful around the house, and was nearing the completion of the rigorous requirements to become an Eagle Scout. Now, all of a sudden, he was getting bad grades (Cs instead of As and Bs), he didn't want to help around the house (certainly not with a good attitude), and he wanted to drop out of Scouts. Dad was devastated. It turned out that his stepson being an Eagle Scout was *his* dream, maybe more than his stepson's.

I suggested to this family that they break the rules. Dad was immediately resistant, while Mom breathed a sigh of relief. The tension in the home was literally making her sick. They relaxed the chores and applauded As, Bs, *and* Cs. They offered their son a break from Eagle Scouts to see if he wanted to "get his head back in the game." When Dad acknowledged to his stepson that his dreams and satisfaction were more important than reaching the goal of Eagle Scout, his stepson began to realize that he really wanted to complete the requirements. Breaking the rules reminded this dad that it wasn't about *his* agenda for his son and reminded the son of what he really did want.

Sometimes our sons cannot grow into a place of "leaving the nest" and taking responsibility for their own lives because we keep them tethered to us with outdated rules or requirements that don't make sense for where they are in their lives. Another boy's experience is all too common. Mitch was not connecting with his dad at all. His father's mode of operation was to say, "I am the father. You are the son. You *will* respect me." In case you hadn't noticed, this approach doesn't work very well with adolescents!

Mitch's dad asked me, "What would *you* do?" (His tone

implied, "with this difficult, hopeless kid.") I suggested that I would back off on my demands for a particular behavior or style of communicating and work instead to foster mutual respect. I would look for something to affirm in Mitch, which would give him permission to begin to tell his story. Rather than beat it into him that he had better not mess up again, I would desperately look for a place of mutuality. That is shoulder-to-shoulder relating. Remember, when the relationship between a parent and teen becomes a power struggle, the parent will always lose.

Mitch's father left my office with a list of five new things to try with his son. For example, instead of immediately saying "no" to something Mitch put in front of him, he was to get as much information as possible by asking three nonjudgmental questions in order to hear his son's heart. Dad was also to recognize and pay more attention to and acknowledge verbally what his son *was* doing rather than what he was not. For example: "I really appreciate the fact that you help clear the table after dinner," or "I saw how you were talking to Mrs. Jacobson, and you really handle yourself well."

Not one hour after Mitch's dad left my office, he paged me, telling me he could not do what I was suggesting for fear his son would run all over him with this new style of parenting. I reassured him that Mitch would welcome the new approach to connecting. Dad went for it, and the response to his efforts has been miraculous. Mitch is showing up and participating; father and son are engaging rather than battling. They still have conflict and differences of opinion, but both Mitch and his dad are developing new skills that keep them focused on their relationship rather than a rule book.

When Breaking the Rules Means Enforcing Them

Chad was a sixteen-year-old sophomore when he started to see me for counseling. He was being raised primarily by a single mom who held joint decision making with her ex-husband. Chad was active in school and church, gifted in singing and acting, and struggling to maintain academic standards. His mom's house rules stated that maintaining less than a B average would result in lost privileges. The problem for Chad was that he had never been "into" academics. (This is a common complaint I hear from boys.) Chad is into the social scene and any opportunities to use his talents for singing and acting.

I have found there is an unspoken rule that often gets written into the fabric of single-parent families. Chad's mom had never been able to hold him to the consequences of his breaking the rules. In her frustration (at Chad and herself) she would throw out a "curse of death" consequence (such as "You'll be grounded until the end of high school," etc.) and, of course, never follow through with it. As a result she was imprisoned by her ultimatums and looked like a fool for not following through. Chad knew that he could break his mom's "rule" about keeping his grades up without paying much of a price. The past for Chad was full of Mom's rescuing him and compensating in areas in which Dad was unable or unwilling to connect. The result was that Chad blamed others and/or his circumstances for difficulties or failures rather than assuming personal responsibility.

As Chad neared the time for performing in his school play, he was not maintaining his B average. He did not hold a lead in this play, but he did have some lines, and the role was important to him. He had made a commitment to the play, people were counting on him, and he was counting on the play. This was where all his passion was focused.

With three weeks to go before the performance, Chad's mom reminded him of the family rule. He was in a panic when he came to his session with me that week because his mom seemed dead serious this time about what the consequence would be: no B average, no school play. When I supported his mom by saying to Chad that she shouldn't have this rule if she didn't intend to keep it, he yelled at me, "*You're* taking the play away from me." My response to Chad was, "*You're* taking the play away from yourself. I love and respect you enough to watch you fail in this one, if that's *your* choice."

Rather than trying to "fix" his dilemma, rescue him, or match his rage with my own, I gave Chad a chance to solve his own problem rather than rely on manipulation to get what he wanted, which was what he had been doing for years. He ranted and raved for a time, which I encouraged. He had a lot to be mad about. He had let himself down by not taking the rules seriously, and his mom had let him down by not taking them seriously either.

Chad came up with a plan to go to each of his teachers and ask what he could do to bring his grades up quickly. He worked very hard to complete the requirements in order to gain *his* reward: participation in the school play. Most important, Chad and his mom learned that Chad can be responsible for his choices and that they are both capable of being held to a higher standard.

When Breaking the Rules *Seems* Like Bad Parenting

When Jeff was seventeen, he told me—with his dad present—about an evening of drinking with friends. After consuming a few beers, Jeff knew that he had a choice to make. He could drive home and risk killing himself or someone else or call his dad and ask for a ride home. He chose the latter.

The spoken rule in this single-parent family is no alcohol consumption until legal age. The rule was already in place for the consequences of drinking—a loss of driving privileges for a time. When Jeff's dad came to pick him up from the party, Jeff was lectured on his poor judgment from the moment he got in the car until they arrived at his bedroom. Jeff repeatedly asked if they could talk about it in the morning, but his dad was unable to break away from his concern and anger and step back from his conviction that this was one of the "teachable moments" that needed to be worked through *now* (even though his son was drunk—not the best context for a "teachable moment"). Because Jeff was under the influence of alcohol and Dad was parenting under the influence of anger, they ended up in a physical conflict, with Dad throwing Jeff on the bed. After a quick tussle they disengaged, but by the time they got to my office for their scheduled appointment the next week, they had barely spoken to each other in days.

During the counseling session I suggested to Jeff's dad that breaking the rules before things blew up would have involved waiting for Jeff to sober up, and taking some time to cool off and think about what would be the most effective way to reach his son. I encouraged Dad (in front of Jeff) that he needed to separate the alcohol issue from the driving issue. I asked Dad to consider affirming Jeff for making a good decision in calling him and asking him for a ride home. I also advocated for Jeff to be included in the decision-making process regarding the length of time he would be without driving privileges.

When Jeff's dad offered what I suggested, I could see Jeff relax as his heart began to reopen a small crack to relationship with his father. Jeff already knew the consequences for drinking. He needed to hear some affirmation for deciding to be honest and responsible by not drinking and driving. *Then* Dad was able to tell Jeff how fearful he was about his behavior, and Jeff was able to process the information well without a conflict. Both father and son apologized, assumed responsibility for their actions, and were able to move forward in connecting despite the intensity of the previous weekend.

Sometimes breaking the rules is staying focused on the *real* issues — not on the half dozen additional issues that come up because of one choice. How do I know what the "real" issue is here for Jeff and his dad? Jeff was reaching out (whenever a teenager does that, *pay attention*), but he was thrown down, squashed, and shamed. Jeff's father didn't know how to communicate under a new set of "rules." He was comfortable with the old rules — good rules against underage drinking. He had not prepared for new rules with a son who was willing to communicate the truth and ask for help. He used the old rules to apply to the new situation, and the result was disconnection. Jeff and his dad will probably need to have several more successful connections before Jeff trusts his dad enough to call him and tell him that he's made a mistake and needs help.

Ending Power Struggles

Patrick's family is another example of what ending the power struggle and opening up communication can look like. It's not easy. Let me warn you—this family went through six months of living hell. Patrick was selfish; he acted out everywhere, drank alcohol whenever he wanted, smoked pot and abused prescription medications, withdrew from sports and hobbies, acted out sexually (in his own bedroom, while his parents were downstairs), and more.

I told Patrick's parents that when kids show up in my office they always get a hug when they come in the door. Why? I inhale whatever smells may linger on them; I make direct eye contact. I confronted Patrick pretty early in the counseling process when he came in for a session. "Why are you drinking in the middle of the day?" I asked him. His initial response was, "Because I can." But after further exploration, I found out just how miserable Patrick was and how desperately he wanted real relationships. He was sad and felt all alone in the world. Drugs, alcohol, and sex were fillers, but he told me they only temporarily made him feel alive. No wonder he was acting out.

I told Patrick's parents they needed to start showing up—smelling their son, looking him in the eye. That's when chaos broke loose, because Patrick felt like he was losing more power. Under the surface the three of them were moving closer, but they didn't know what to do when they got there. So they just got in each other's faces.

There is no such thing as "eight steps to a happy teenager." Parenting teens is messy. We make mistakes. Our teenagers make it hard. We parents are prone to react. But when we react, we are not shoulder to shoulder, and we will not connect with our son. And when we are not connecting with him, our disconnection can shove him into a world that could destroy him.

Patrick's dad eventually came in with his son for a session. They sat down, Patrick straight and tall, his dad directly across from him. At once his father began to tell me everything Patrick was doing wrong. I watched as Patrick sank lower and lower into my couch. Finally, I interrupted Dad. "Any strengths?" I asked from my seat positioned diagonally from Patrick.

"Don't interrupt me," his dad barked.

I interrupted immediately. "We start out with the positive here. Patrick knows he's here because he keeps messing up. I don't want our initial connection to be focused on the negative."

Patrick sat up on the couch. I was challenging the system and modeling the beginning of shoulder-to-shoulder communication. Dad wasn't ready for the shift.

In a furious tirade Patrick's father lashed out at me. I felt all the anger and frustration that had been directed at Patrick for years. The frustration came from not knowing how to connect with his son.

I looked at Patrick's dad, who I knew was scared and certain that the only way he would "get his son under control" was to be in his face and in my face. Calmly and firmly I said, "One more outburst, and you'll be out of here."

If possible, Patrick sat up even straighter. From the side he saw someone who was interested in what might be really important: what was inside of him, not just his outside behaviors.

Nevertheless, not too long after that difficult session I got an emergency page and learned that Patrick was threatening to kill himself. SWAT was called in. When I arrived at the house, Mom was in the kitchen talking with an officer, and Dad was in the main part of the house talking to another officer. Patrick was locked in his bedroom.

Did he really want to die? When I got to talk to him, I heard his angst about wanting some control and feeling like he was losing it all. He was certain his parents weren't willing to deviate from their perspective or their way of doing things. He felt like giving up.

After Patrick and I talked for a while and I determined that he was not at risk of killing himself that night, SWAT left, and Patrick and I and his parents were able to roundtable. We talked about what was happening, what had gone wrong, and where they needed to go from here. Every family needs to do this often. I asked Patrick's family to pay attention to the big picture—what they and Patrick really wanted for his life. His parents wanted Patrick to participate and succeed at school, clean up from drugs and alcohol, get his anger in check, and do a better job at communicating his angst. Patrick said he wanted to be a better communicator, have significant relationships, connect more with his dad, graduate from high school, and have a plan for the future.

The four of us then made a list of the steps Patrick needed to take to reach his goals. I asked his mom and dad to break their old rules in some areas and let Patrick be seventeen years old. That meant letting him succeed *and* fail. Some of their expectations regarding his performance needed to change, as did their hyperfocus on what he "looked like" on the outside lately—his poor grades and drug use, for example. Patrick expressed how overwhelmed he felt by so many of the things he wanted to do well. He really wanted his parents' support and trust and to know they loved him and believed in him.

After a few hours of developing a concrete strategy that could make this kind of connection possible, I went home and crashed. In the weeks and months that followed, I watched Patrick and his parents work hard to connect and pursue each other. I feel that his parents' willingness to focus more on their relationship with their son than on his behavior was the key to turning Patrick's story around. Some rule breaking on their part not only ended a power struggle and opened communication, but probably saved their son's life.

Now Patrick is twenty-four, has graduated from college, is in a good relationship, and has a job (even though he has had a few earrings as well!). His parents are still together (they decided to get on the same page to keep from not only destroying their relationship with their son, but with each other). Mom was always the more malleable one. Dad had to stretch to break a few rules in order to save his son, but this also enabled him to listen to his wife more often. He actually felt relief at learning it was not his role to be in control of everything. Their other children have given them challenges as well, but they have changed how they relate to their children while changing some of the family rules.

Taking a Break, Giving a Break

Because I have found that breaking the rules is one of the most effective strategies in capturing the heart of a teenage boy, I'm going to offer you several other examples of families that took a break from doing things the old way. I encourage you to keep in mind the element of surprise that can inject into your family dynamic just what is missing in a system that's simply not working. What do you really have to lose?

SCHOOL. I work with a family who has a thirteen-year-old and a fourteen-year-old. Three weeks from school's end, the younger son was failing two classes and his brother was failing one. They had been threatened with repeating grades, being grounded all summer, and losing all privileges through high school (the "curse of death" is at work in reaction to failure in this family). I suggested they make signs that simply read D- and post them all over the house. I urged the teens to "kick butt" for three weeks, talk to teachers, do whatever it took to *pass* those classes. We planned to talk about strategies to stay out of this dilemma in the future, but for the moment, we broke the rules and did everything to encourage these kids to pass. The goal: Show them that their parents are *for* them and will help them *through* failure rather than abandon them *to* it.

Before you worry that I encouraged these parents to "enable" their children's failures, let me say that I have seen far too many kids in middle school get into an academic "hole" that they can't get out of, and it haunts them throughout the rest of school, leading some to drop out. Middle school is the time to do everything possible to give your kids some success. That's not enabling—that's securing a future. Traditional school doesn't work for some guys. If your son is one of them, look into alternative schools. If it's late in the game, look at a GED. Once again, *look* for a context for success, even if it means breaking traditional rules.

Consider breaking the rules by giving your son one "ditch day" a quarter during the school year. Go snowboarding or play paintball together. Ask your son what *he* thinks would be a fun way to "waste" time together. When I do activities with the guys I counsel, you should see the sheer joy on their faces. They get it. I'm taking time away from my other responsibilities, and we're not just toeing the line, even in counseling. I'm showing up in their lives and giving them a break from the rules. Why? Because *they* matter more than the rules do.

CHURCH. A lot of teenagers get bored with church and don't want their parents' religion. This can be a good thing because they really do need to establish their faith for themselves. I give guys permission to not be in sync spiritually if that's where they are. This is far better than pretending or growing to hate anything spiritual. I also understand parents who want their families in church together as part of a family experience. Breaking the rules might mean giving your son one or two passes a month to miss church.

CHORES. There are a lot of issues to confront during adolescence. I am often amazed when parents want to spend a good sum of money for counseling because their son's backpack is constantly left in the living room; or he won't pick up his towel after he showers; or he keeps "forgetting" to make his bed or take out the garbage. Fighting about this kind of minutia takes up a lot of space and leaves little room for the issues of significance. I'm not suggesting you let your kids run the house or do nothing to help out. But try to be *creative*, always remembering that your long-term goal is to capture your son's *heart*, not control his will.

You might collect stuff he's strewn throughout the house, toss it in a basket, and let him know it will go to the Goodwill on Friday. This can't be a "curse of death" threat, but a natural consequence that is calmly carried out, leaving room to deal with more important issues. If the trash has not been put out in a timely manner, then place it all in the middle of your son's room and close the door. I guarantee he will never forget, and you will have fun hauling all the bags and baskets to his room.

One last piece of advice: Let his room be *his* room. Let him keep the mess if he insists. Unless something is actually dying or growing in there, give him (and yourself) a break.

HYGIENE. A lot of younger adolescent boys are lax (to say the least) when it comes to personal hygiene. This is a place where you can take a break and trust them to move. They will eventually. I promise. Budget for a dermatologist or Crest Whitestrips and then wait. It's just a matter of time. However, if you assert your agenda, they will take longer getting there.

And how much does it matter if your sixteen-year-old has blue hair? Is hair really a big deal? I promise he won't have blue hair when he's thirty-four. Surprising your son by not making a big deal over small, temporary whims can be a powerful way to connect with him.

One of my clients, Chase, has naturally red hair. I mean *really* red hair. He hated it, but his parents flatly refused to allow him to dye it; in their eyes (not Chase's) his red hair was something to be prized. The "no dye" rule was just one of a litany of regulations Chase was expected to conform to. All of his fights with his parents (with his dad in particular) were about rules. In Chase's father's linear approach to parenting — making it all about rules, structure, and doing the "right" things — he lost connection with his son, who was all about heart, sensitivity, and telling stories. Chase's mom tried to make up for his dad. She would either make excuses for Dad's inflexibility or talk negatively about his rigidness. This sent a mixed message to Chase about whether Dad was a good guy or a bad guy, which makes a young man wonder whether his own maleness is good or bad. As a result Chase acted out — he became aggressive, hostile, bored, and disconnected. He was a kid set up to be in trouble.

When I began to work with Chase, I made a deal with him. I said, "No more fights. Call me before you get into an altercation, and I'll fight for you to change your hair color." Over time Chase's mom began to get a new perspective that allowed her to see beyond his "prized" red hair (to her) and to understand where his heart was really at. The work with Chase and his dad was slower. I remember the session when things began to turn around. Chase told his dad, with tears streaming down his face, "I don't think you love me." I didn't let Dad move in with a lecture or a listing of all he'd done for Chase. I wanted him to *hear* his son, not react to him. I calmly said, "You'll sit with him in that." That was a beginning.

Three months later Chase's parents let him dye his hair brown. Nothing bad happened as a result. After four months of dying it, Chase let his natural hair color come back. I think this was due to how his parents joined him in his process rather than asserting their "rules" above all else.

MUSIC. When your son has a bad day, *encourage* him to listen to his music. You might even *really* break the rules and tell him to crank up the volume, as long as it doesn't bother the neighbors. You can get a pair of earplugs.

Better yet, you can surprise the heck out of your son by actually *listening* to his music with him. Music is a great escape from the realities of what life throws at us. Often music speaks to our inner struggles via lyrics. We know that someone else can understand. In my late adolescence and early adulthood I was very much a part of the heavy-metal, hard-rock scene. I went to concerts, I knew all the lyrics to my favorite bands' songs, and I recognized that the music resonated with how I felt inside at the time: angry.

Maybe your son likes heavy metal or rap; he's feeding himself a steady diet of angry, aggressive music, and you're really nervous about it. Rather than trying to ban all his music from your house, go out of your way to listen to it. Don't make any comments on it. Just listen. Be with him while he emotes through listening to music. This shows him that you can handle his emotions, that he doesn't have to keep them all inside where they can take him captive. Try dialoguing (not monologuing) with your son about lyrics you find especially troublesome. Ask him why he thinks music that expresses "I'll kill you before you kill me" is important in our culture. Where does this sense of despair come from? Create a conversation about injustice, racism, frustration, and disrespect. You will be modeling to him another way to deal with all those emotions—open communication. That is the good thing about music—it communicates emotions. The best use of your son's music is to continue that communication about emotions (not about how bad the music is and what your son should or shouldn't be feeling). You might actually connect with your son's heart in the process, and that would make sorting through all the "garbage" worthwhile.

Demonstrating Flexibility

The goal in taking a break from what is familiar for you and giving your kid a break is demonstrating that you are willing to be flexible in order to connect with your son. When parenting a teen, sometimes the best you can hope for is to feel uncomfortable. Yes, uncomfortable! Because we simply don't always have the "right" answers or rules, or the way we apply them is meeting with nothing but yawning or yelling. When that's the case, it's time to take a break and even say, "I don't know what to say or do right now, but I'll get back to you in a few hours."

I have a friend who picked her daughter up from an out-of-control party one night, and her son called her on her way home from work the next day to confess he'd been caught smoking marijuana at school. She wisely told each of them in the moment, "We'll talk about this later, when I'm not so mad and scared." Breaking the rules is realizing that everything does not have to be hashed out and resolved *right now* (that's impossible anyway). As parents we often think if we can get to the bottom of things and dispense wisdom and tighter regulations, we've done a good job. Usually, however, we've just given ourselves an illusion of control and given our kids the idea that they'd better work really hard next time not to get caught.

One mom I worked with summarized her parenting journey eloquently:

Raising my son has definitely been a struggle. How do I save him from a dad who doesn't see him like I do? How do I rescue him from a school that doesn't appreciate him like I do? How do I protect him from a peer group that doesn't include him like I want them to? How do I keep him from friends who don't encourage him the way I think they should? How do I guard him from the pain of failure in today's world?

The answer that I'm learning (over and over and over again) is . . . I don't.

My goal has become, instead, to *love him well*. Do I love him enough to let him fall? Do I love him enough to let *him* figure it out? Do I love him enough to understand and listen, instead of save . . . to support instead of rescue . . . to encourage instead of protect . . . to walk with instead of guard . . . to believe in instead of discourage . . . to see him for who he is instead of who he isn't?

Yes, it's a struggle, but it's also a privilege, an honor, and a blessing.

When parents can break the rules for the betterment of their children, it shows that their highest priority is their child. That can turbocharge even the toughest relationship with fresh life and unity. And then *the chase is on*.

GO FOR IT!

ON YOUR MARKS!

Sit down with your spouse or a good friend and honestly write out the rules you have for your son—spoken and unspoken. Also ask your son to write out what *he* believes the rules to be. During a time when you're not in conflict with each other, discuss which rules are appropriate and which rules might need to change. Let this be a conversation of give-and-take and negotiation. Highlight what you are willing to be flexible on. As you consider the rules, ask yourself: "What motivates these rules—fear or love?" When we parent out of fear, we cannot think clearly. When we parent out of love, we are drawn to our *son*, not to the rules.

GET SET!

Make a "hot list" of ways, given your evolving set of rules, you're going to handle and respond to every situation that might come up. It's far easier to deal with a crisis when you've prepared.

GO!

Using this chapter as a springboard, sit with your spouse (if you are together) and come up with five tools that you could consistently follow in stirring it up with your son. Focus specifically on doing something different in your approach to parenting. For example, you could express willingness to negotiate a later curfew, or let go of always having to be the first one to talk or the last one to be heard.

5

The Deal with Drugs

Matthew, age sixteen, was an average student who sometimes earned Bs and even an A occasionally when a subject grabbed his intelligent but often apathetic mind. He was a nice kid, and he didn't really have any "problems." He was a good big brother to twelve-year-old Katie and went to church regularly.

Matthew came to see me for counseling two days after being admitted to the emergency room for alcohol poisoning. He had a blood alcohol level of .379—almost five times the legal limit in most states and a potentially lethal level. Matthew's parents had no idea that their son even drank. He was lucky that he didn't die or suffer any organ damage. The American Psychological Association defines binge drinking as consuming five alcoholic drinks in an hour. Matthew thought he had probably consumed sixteen shots in about a ninety-minute timeframe. In my conversation with him I asked him what his intention was when he was getting ready to go out that night. He told me that he needed to show his friends that he could keep up with the other guys. He said, "My popularity was riding on that night."

Remember, boys are looking to create their own story—a story that connects them to something of value and prestige, something that elevates them and gives them status, what Ron Taffel in *The Second Family* calls "the currency of cool." Guys like Matthew do dumb and even potentially deadly things because they think it's their only chance to pocket this invaluable commodity.

What's one of the most extreme things you've done in your life to look cool? When I was twenty-two, I scaled a six-story hotel to steal a flag. That was really dumb, but I did something that connected with the other guys. At seventeen, Andrew was the first one at a party to smoke crystal methamphetamine. When I asked him why he chose to do that, he said he wanted his girlfriend and his buddies to think he was a rebel—someone who was willing to be the "wild man." One consequence of that night's choice was that Andrew became addicted, and the drug ruled his life for seven years. Another of my clients jumped into a swimming pool at the beginning of summer camp with all his clothes (and boots) on. He was in trouble before camp began, but he connected with the other kids.

When your kids do foolish or dangerous things, can you connect with their stories? Is there a part of you that remembers being so desperate to belong? I later learned that in reality Matthew was not really close to being "in" with the illusive popular group, but he desperately wanted to be because of the status they held. Like most adolescents, Matthew longed to be a part of something cool. He believed that if he didn't drink as much as or more than the rest his peers, he didn't have a chance of fitting in. He was willing to risk a lot to belong—to feel connected.

A Dose of Reality

I cannot emphasize this point enough: *Kids drink alcohol*—a lot of alcohol. Kids smoke pot. Some smoke daily. Kids abuse your prescription medications and theirs. They reach into the cabinets at your friends' homes and take their meds too. Kids experiment and abuse over-the-counter drugs like Robitussin, Coricidin, and NyQuil—all of which contain a chemical called dextromethorphan (DXM). Access to these nonprescription drugs is easy and the cost is cheap. I could flag down a teen at the local suburban high school and ask where I could score some bud (marijuana), mushrooms (hallucinogens), or ecstasy, and in one hour have whatever I requested, even though I am an adult.

Drugs are in our schools, church youth groups, athletic programs, and all other extracurricular activities. J. P., age seventeen, regularly attends youth group—not for spiritual reasons, but to buy pot from the church dealer. About drugs J. P. says, "Just the mention of the word freaks parents out. Kids, though, start to drool. Even the 'good kids.'" This may seem hard to believe, but it's happening. Drugs and alcohol are everywhere, and your kids are being impacted by the effects socially, behaviorally, emotionally, and spiritually.

Most of the guys I work with have incredible spirits. They can be passionate and alive in certain areas but feel so insecure in social settings and relationships that they just want to shut down. Having an underdeveloped sense of self can lead to self-medicating. Being authentic and real in a society that does not encourage teenage boys or men to participate in an authentic emotional life can also lead to self-medicating. Bottom line: To connect, cope, and find relief, many boys choose alcohol and drugs.

My friend and fellow counselor, Sharon Hersh, in her excellent book on girls and substance abuse, *"Mom, Everyone Else Does!"*, writes about the first time she let her daughter have friends over for a party while she was out for the evening. When she got home to a house reeking of alcohol and cigarettes, she was stunned. "I might have been naive before this night," Sharon wrote, "but I had a permanent mark on my coffee table to remind me that teenagers don't pop popcorn and watch movies anymore."

She asked her fourteen-year-old daughter, "Kristin, what happened tonight?"

"Mom," her daughter said, "I'm not sure. This is what kids do. This happens *all the time*."

My friend quickly responded, "Well, if this is what happens all the time, you're not going out again or having anyone over. No more parties!"

Kristin looked her mom right in the eyes, and with tears streaming down her face, she said, "Mom, if you want me to stay away from drugs and drinking, then I can't go anywhere—not even to school. It's what everyone does—all the time."[3]

Your son may be smoking pot or binge drinking. He may be sneaking alcohol from a liquor cabinet at your house or a friend's. He may be smoking cigarettes or experimenting with alcohol and marijuana at parties or in the car on the way to school, at the bus stop, in the backyard late at night while everyone is asleep, at the local park while little kids are playing, before sporting events. Do you know what signs to look for? (See the appendix if you need some tips.) Are you afraid to know what is *really* going on? Are you parenting with your eyes wide open?

Under the Influence

Today's kids choose to be overstimulated by entertainment, video games, cell phones, pornography, and substance abuse. Drugs and alcohol temporarily fill a void—a void of belonging, relational connection, success in an area of personal passion, or a sense of being "okay" in a pretty tough world.

David, age eighteen, calls alcohol "liquid courage." He and other boys tell me that drugs and alcohol help them forget about the stress they are experiencing. We need to be careful not to dismiss their anxiety. Adolescence is one of the most stressful times of life. And remember, we talked about teenage boys being like Crock-Pots. They stuff a lot of emotions and tension inside and keep their internal temperature at a slow simmer. Often one issue for a teen will get magnified into all the other areas of his life, filling the "Crock-Pot" to the brim. Alcohol helps boys release some of the pressure in the pot. Unfortunately, it also hijacks their brains so that their bodies eventually become unable to deal with stress in a normal way.

Teenagers (especially boys) are not trained to pay attention to anything. Boys are learning most of what they know about how to "be" in the world from their friends, who are not educated in truth or reality when it comes to substance use and abuse. It is cool to be "chill" and just see what happens. They do not pay attention to their consumption of alcohol or drugs or know why they even want or eventually need to drink. *Need* to drink? My clients tell me all the time that alcohol loosens them up, fills their pockets with the "currency of cool," helps them hook up with girls, and makes them feel like one of the guys. Those are pretty powerful needs, which explain why alcohol use is considered a *necessity* by most teenage boys in social settings.

When teens tell me that alcohol is the best medicine for connection in their social scene, I tell them that it really just makes them a social chameleon. Alcohol and drugs allow them to disconnect from themselves—not care about their anxiety, values, inhibitions, or true desires—so they can just "go with the flow." This disconnection justifies the means (drinking), but ultimately leaves them empty, longing for real connection but believing it will only happen if they are under the influence.

When Parents Are Part of the Problem

I recall my first meeting with a fifteen-year-old client whose mom had picked him up from a friend's house and smelled beer on his breath. She brought him in to see me, hoping I would give her the seven steps to keeping her son away from alcohol. Instead I asked her, "Do you really think you will be able to keep your son from alcohol?"

"Yes," she answered emphatically.

"Then you'll need to take him out of school," I said. I was surprised to see a tear roll down her son's cheek. I was validating what he already knew—that alcohol is everywhere in the teen world. No parent can keep their kid from the temptation.

That doesn't mean you are completely powerless when it comes to influencing your son's use of drugs and alcohol. In this chapter we will look at some proactive and positive ways you can be involved. But first, take a look at the questionnaire below to see where you are in your beliefs about substance abuse among teens. What parenting style are you most inclined to use if your son is seduced by alcohol or drugs?

1. Do you see the war on drugs as something that impacts other families or as something that might be going on in your own home?
2. What is your immediate reaction to the statement, "Everyone does it"?
3. Do you allow your children to drink in your home?
4. Do you lock your own alcohol away from your children?
5. Does your own alcohol use impact your children?
6. When you hear stories about your son's friends who use drugs or alcohol, do you use this information against him (i.e., keep him from socializing with these friends)?
7. Do you believe that you can or should know everything that is going on in your teenager's life?
8. If you learned that your son was using drugs or alcohol, would you tell anyone outside the family?
9. If you learned that your son was using drugs or alcohol, would it change your feelings about him?
10. Have you established family rules for consequences of drinking or using drugs, or are you hoping this doesn't occur? If it does, are you bracing yourself to "come down hard" on your son to keep it from happening again?

Permissive Parents

One of the reasons that alcohol permeates adolescent life is that some parents have decided it is better to provide a "safe" environment for their teens to use substances, since they're going to use them anyway. Lisa and Charlie have four children; two are teen boys, ages fifteen and eighteen. They are a tight family unit. They support each other by attending sibling sporting events and other extracurricular activities. The family rule is no alcohol until you are of legal age. Steven (the eighteen-year-old) recently graduated from high school. He has been experimenting with alcohol without his parents' knowledge. Steven has a strong opinion that he should be able to drink. He justifies his cause because his best friend's parents provide a "safe" environment for the boys to drink responsibly in their home. They also provide the alcohol.

Permissive parents are doing great harm to parents who attempt to have a consistent family plan, and they send a very confusing message to teenagers. A permissive parent is one who justifies in his or her mind, *kids are going to drink, so we'll provide a "safe" place.* I believe this is a parent who doesn't have the courage to stand firm for his son. Permissiveness is a gateway to other unacceptable behaviors. If you give permission to young people to break the law because you are looking to connect with your son, then you are also giving them permission to be manipulative and to hide behaviors like pornography use and sexual relationships.

In the moment permissive parents really look cool. In the end they are still disconnected. Permission to break the law and to practice potentially harmful behaviors in your home is toxic glue to connect with your son. A teen won't pursue you to be an ally and guide, because he doesn't respect you. Teenage boys are looking anywhere and everywhere to justify at-risk behaviors, and they will justify using drugs and alcohol because they've watched you condone their use.

Controlling Parents

Often when parents get the wake-up call that their son is using drugs or alcohol, they go to the other end of the continuum. They may strip their son's room of all his belongings, make him get a job or do volunteer work, ban all peer relationships, or require daily Bible studies. Although some of these responses may be appropriate, when they are motivated by a determination to control the son, parents enter into a power struggle they will lose. Power and control issues lead to issues with self-esteem. When parents try to control their son, it is hard for him to believe that there is much good in him. Issues with self-esteem always lead to self-medicating (whatever form that may take), which leads to disconnection from parents, which can fuel more power and control issues.

Fear of the unknown can grip us and lock us in a cage of desperation. Families with adolescents who experiment with or use and abuse drugs tell me they feel like they are walking in a fog. Many of my clients come from other drug and alcohol programs that place them in front of a video that attempts to educate them about substance abuse. Let's get real here. Kids use and abuse drugs and alcohol to connect to something, usually people, particularly their peers. Boys are looking for a relationship, and drugs and alcohol initially promise to be a great friend to those who feel like they can't connect or have proven to themselves that they are not good at feeling at home in the adolescent world. Freaked-out parents and "just say no" education is not powerful enough to overcome this seductive promise of entry into "belonging" in the adolescent world.

What's a Parent to Do?

Philip was seventeen years old and addicted to cocaine. He used coke by himself, away from friends and family. He used almost daily in his bedroom. His parents didn't have any idea about his habit. Before you judge them too harshly, let me say that this type of use can be easy to miss. Cocaine boosts some kids' energy level. They look how they're "supposed" to look—they study, keep their room clean, go to practice. When a kid is struggling with low-level depression that is sometimes part of adolescent life, or he has a personality type that is not high-energy, cocaine seems like the perfect medicine. Parents are relieved that their son is energetic and doing things, and are often unaware that a potentially lethal substance is responsible for this "positive" change.

The mom of one of my clients told me about finding out that her son used drugs and alcohol: "Kevin got caught at a church retreat smoking pot. I will never forget that moment. Talk about being blindsided. We knew Kev experimented with alcohol, but we had no idea that he was drinking and smoking so *much*."

What's a parent to do in this tricky world where substance use and abuse often sneak up on the family? The most important thing to do is to calmly focus on the truth and begin to uncover the distorted thought processes that are holding your son prisoner to poor choices.

Stinking Thinking

Distorted thought processes can come from the media, from parents' relationship with drugs and alcohol, or from peers, but these thought patterns actually carve a rut in your son's brain that provides him justification for using. You've got to be willing to persevere and carve another rut that will eventually empower your son to make different choices.

Here are some of the distorted thoughts I've heard from adolescent boys:

- Beer/pot doesn't hurt me.
- Pot keeps me motivated and successful.
- Marijuana is even legal in some countries.
- In order to socialize or hook up with girls, I have to be drunk/buzzed.
- If I don't smoke cigarettes, then I won't be able to handle the stress.
- If I don't smoke pot or drink, I will not fit in or have fun.
- If I don't use drugs with other kids, they won't think I'm cool.

An adolescent's brain gets stuck in the rut of distorted thought processes because the culture (and sometimes his parents) preach that illegal alcohol and drug use is socially acceptable. What needs to be fed is the esteem of the adolescent. I ask my guys many questions. Here are a few:

1. Why do you need to drink?
2. Whom are you trying to impress?
3. What do you really get out of the party scene?
4. How do you view yourself while drinking/drugging?
5. Are you proud of your view?
6. How do you feel the next morning?
7. Have you gotten comfortable with feeling guilty and feeling terrible physically?
8. Would your future wife like to see you in this scene?

A teenager needs to know that you are stronger than he is, but he also needs to know that you can handle whatever he throws at you with compassion, consistency, and even a sense of humor. This combination meets the deepest needs of a teenager's heart—to be known, accepted, forgiven, and still wanted. As you persevere in talking about the distorted thought patterns, resist the urge to preach, lecture, or be disgusted by your son's poor choices. Practice with your spouse or a friend. Be creative. Have a sense of humor.

The mom of one of my clients was concerned about her son's habit of using a whole can of chewing tobacco daily. He spits into used plastic soda bottles. For a month she saved his bottles, and for Christmas she poured all of his spit into a clear five-gallon jug, wrapped it up, and put it under the tree with the rest of her son's gifts. Sounds disgusting! But it was a great visual to her son about what he was putting in his body every month. She recently told me that since the first of the year he has not chewed once. I laughed because I tell the parents I work with that sometimes you have to do something shocking to get your kid's attention. This mom did!

The big question to consider is this: If your son knew — I mean really knew — that he is valuable, smart, funny, likeable, sensitive, etc., would he need to act out of the distorted thinking listed above? One hundred percent of my clients say, "No."

After working with one eighteen-year-old for three years, he finally got it — that he was valuable, smart, funny, and likeable. He got it by being able to share his stories with me without being condemned. He got it because I never gave the message that his substance abuse was no big deal, but I continually hammered home the fact that *he* was a big deal. He got it because his mother persevered in sending the same messages. By the time he graduated from high school, he was done with the distorted thoughts that justified his substance use. He recently brought to a therapy session a CD from one of his favorite artists, Matisyahu. Matisyahu is a Jewish reggae singer who was at one time addicted to cocaine. He certainly gets it when it comes to substance abuse. My client told me he loved the lyric from one of the songs: "You can be so high and feel so low." Now that's some clear thinking that will continue to help this young man make good choices and create positive self-esteem.

Does Your Son Know You Like Him?

As I was transitioning from adolescence to early adulthood, I knew I needed to talk to a man about my life. I think a lot of boys experience this passage into adulthood with a desire to talk to a man — sometimes other than their father — about what it means to be a man. The man I picked challenged me to look at the choices I was making in my life and the distorted thought patterns that supported some of these choices. He simply asked, "Are you convicted by any of your choices?"

My first reaction was, "No. Why would I be?" I thought I was living the dream life. I was a good athlete, seemed to be attractive to girls, and all my peers were encouraging my choices.

This wise mentor asked me to take six weeks and ask myself, *Should I be convicted about any of my choices?* For him it was not about moral judgments or following rules or conforming to his agenda. Nevertheless, his request set off an internal conflict. I began to challenge every choice I made and discovered that although I was living the "dream life," I was not present to myself. I was not in touch with my emotions, passions, desires, or disappointments. The main thing I used to disconnect was anger — and acting my anger out. I also engaged in stealing. During the brief moments of acting out either behavior, I could escape dealing with anything about my personal reality that I didn't know how to handle. As I kept my mentor's challenge in the forefront of my mind for a period of time, I found myself convicted, and I wanted to run from the truth of the person I was becoming. But I couldn't. I had found a man who cared enough about me to connect with my heart. He liked me and wanted me to like myself.

Most teenagers work hard to not be present with themselves. That's usually because they've internalized what they don't like about themselves—they've acted awkward, rebellious, moody, and aggressive, and they've been told how undesirable these qualities are. Why bother to be present to someone you're already sure is not very likeable?

When adolescents act out by using drugs and alcohol, they are not very likable. We must separate their behaviors from them. If our sons feel like we don't like them, there is no chance they will like themselves. This becomes a vicious cycle. They will self-medicate to deal with their self-contempt, which makes them less likable, which fuels their self-contempt, which makes self-medication with drugs and/or alcohol seem justifiable. If you want to join the drug war on behalf of your son, here is the most important thing you can do: *Let him know you like him!*

I recently took my three-year-old son to the park. All the way there he asked me repeatedly, "Daddy, do you like me?" That is the question our boys are asking, whether they say it out loud or not. They know we love them—that's what parents are *supposed* to do. But do we like them?

I have a wonderful window of opportunity with my young children right now to let them know how much I like them. I was delighted that my little man was so interested in engaging with me. In response to his question, I told him that I loved him; he looked at me intently and asked again, "But do you *like* me?" I emphatically told him that I *reeeaaalllly* liked him. Our time at the park seemed so different from usual because we had connected in a new way.

All the way through high school I would come home to my

mom and cookies or a sandwich, and she'd say, "How was your day?" Day after day of her waiting for me warmed me up to tell her my stories. Mom would also take me to countless swim practices (and she would listen to *my* music while we were in the car—Guns N' Roses at the time). My mom could name the song, hum along, and even sing some of the lyrics. Did she love the music? No. But I knew she not only loved me, but liked me. Listening to my music showed me that she wanted to know me. She saw my soul through those car rides, and she let me know that she liked what she saw.

But what do you do when your son's behaviors are not very likable? What if your older son is shut down? He's not asking if you like him, because he's already concluded that you probably don't. You may not like that he smells, his room smells, his clothes smell, and he tries to cover it up with deodorant. Boys are messy. You might not like the choices he's been making lately. But letting him know that you like *him* no matter what—that there is nothing, absolutely nothing he can do to make you stop liking him—may literally save his life.

Corey, age fifteen, sauntered into my office with an air of arrogance. His mom and dad followed, downtrodden and dejected. In our first session it was clear that these parents did not have one positive thing to say about their son. They focused only on the negative: drug abuser, habitual liar, failure in school, misfit in social situations. Corey has three siblings who toe the line and are the exact opposite of him. Both parents are highly educated professionals in respected fields. This family was disconnected and disjointed, and nothing was working in their interactions with their second child.

In the weeks ahead I received phone calls and emergency pages to crisis event after crisis event, including Corey's arrest for theft and possession of illegal substances. His parents told me repeatedly how much they hated their son. They wanted him out of the house and out of their lives forever. The first time they told me this, tears welled up in my eyes as I thought about this wounded young man. Corey's parents looked at each other in shock; I think they were guessing I would totally agree with them that he was to be hated. Instead I told them how much sorrow I felt at hearing that they had lost the desire to be close to their son.

Two years have passed since the initial session, and Corey is now set to graduate from high school and is going to college. He has been sober and clean from all illicit substances for more than a year. He knows who he is today, and he continues to make progress with integrity and character. He has a small, solid group of friends, and his relationship with his family is the strongest it has ever been. His father has worked harder than any father I have known. He came to weekly therapy sessions and spent hours pinpointing the ways his son's behavior triggered him, so he could come up with ways to combat his first reaction and respond in ways that created connection. Dad was amazing with putting his hurt, frustration, and anger on the back burner. In doing so, he empowered himself to *see* his son and engage with his heart.

We have had to be very flexible and creative in this case, as Corey was like a robot repeatedly bumping into a wall but never trying a new path. The robot needed a new program; Corey needed to know that his world and relationships and circumstances could all dramatically improve if he showed up and participated. Because of the progress Corey saw in his dad, he started working hard at making changes. It has been amazing for me to watch and participate in the incredible healing that has occurred in this family.

Open Heart, Open Home

Like this visionary and dedicated dad, you can learn to pursue your son with persistence and continuity to convey to him that you like him—and that he is worth something in this world. Here are some more ideas to keep your heart and home open to your son and increase your chances of weathering the storm of teenage substance abuse.

KEEP COMMUNICATION OPEN. Don't condemn, freak out, or overreact if your son is drinking or drugging. Talk openly about what he is doing. Ask questions to learn about him, not to set the conversation up for your prepackaged lecture. Ask questions that allow him to tell you what is true in his world. Don't shut him down. Whether or not you agree or understand, tell yourself, *He really means this.* That is, *He is really in touch with his thoughts right now and is making a choice to express those thoughts to me.* Unless this happens, there can be no meaningful connection. So encourage your son to bring it on. Letting him know that you are not afraid of his story emulates how teenagers support each other by asking questions and actively listening. I have learned a lot by watching the way teenage friends interact with each other. Because they have been shoulder to shoulder in so many social and relational circumstances, they have earned each other's permission to connect face-to-face. As a result they generally make good eye contact. They are expressive with each other. They *hear* rather than lecture each other. They intuitively know how to keep communication with each other open and flowing. You can learn to do the same with your son.

GET EDUCATED. Facts are good and necessary in the context of connectedness. You need to know more about alcohol and substance abuse than your son does. That means you need to educate yourself about what is going on in your son's culture, *right now.* I encourage parents to go online and find the most current information on what drugs are most popular with teens and how much alcohol they consume. Know what your son faces every day and talk openly about it. Oh, and don't expect your son to immediately respond to the facts with, "Thank you so much, Mom, for telling me this. I didn't know. I'll never drink again." His first response is likely to be defensive and argumentative, mostly because he has been flushed out of his secret world by a savvy mom or dad. I coach parents that the way they approach their son and preface the conversation will have a lot to do with the way he responds.

Michael's dad came to me because he was suspicious of what his sixteen-year-old son was up to on weekends. He had told Michael that if he ever caught him smoking pot or drinking alcohol, Michael would never get a car or hang out with his friends ever again — for as long as he lived under his dad's roof. But Dad suspected that his son was partying anyway, and he came to me exasperated. "How can I find out what Michael is up to?" he asked.

I told him to get educated about substances first, as he had never been a big drinker and had not used illicit drugs of any kind. He was shocked with the information he obtained about pot and what it does to the brain and body, as well as about how many of today's teens are abusing alcohol. He was ready to approach his son about what he was learning, so I explained to Michael that his dad had been working hard to understand his world in an attempt to connect with him. In their next session together I was amazed at how open Michael was, not only to hearing the information his dad brought to the table but also to vulnerably admitting that he was struggling with pot and alcohol. Michael did not receive any consequence at that time—only a huge hug from his dad, who told him how grateful he was for his son's honesty and willingness to share. Within the next six months Michael amazed me even more by asking his dad for support and accountability to help keep him clean and sober. Dad continues to educate himself about exactly what Michael is dealing with, and his empathetic approach has connected him to his son in awesome ways.

DON'T JUSTIFY, MINIMIZE, OR ENABLE. I worked with one boy whose father responded to his experimentation with marijuana by telling his son that he had likewise experimented when he was younger and that it was no big deal. Remember, this is about your son, not you. For teenagers today, experimenting with drugs and alcohol can be a *very* big deal. Our job as parents is to dig and get to what is true for our son while challenging his distorted thought processes.

A lot of my clients will ask me if I have used drugs or alcohol. I always ask them what their motivation is in asking the question. They will often tell me that they just want to connect with me. I respond, "Even if we don't relate on everything, we can still connect." I find that boys in particular often use adults' self-disclosure to justify their own use of drugs and alcohol. I don't believe there is a need for us to share our experiences or make up a story of drug or alcohol use in order to connect. Spending time and communicating with your son is what connects you. Every opportunity to talk about drugs and alcohol is a savored moment (whether your son lets on to this or not). Hearing your son's thoughts and experiences will encourage him to eventually ask you what your thoughts are. Earning the right to be heard takes hours of listening to your son. Too often parents self-disclose for their own benefit—to get something off their chest or to appear cool. If there is a history of addiction in your family, at some point you will need to disclose it. You will need to evaluate whether your son can process this information and how much he can process. Before you share, however, you might need a third party's opinion as to whether what you're planning to tell him is really for your child's good.

STAY TUNED IN. Start paying more attention to what your son is doing. If he is sleeping over at a friend's every Friday night, it may be a sign that he is drinking to excess and wants to sober up before you see him. If I were you, I just might show up really late at the friend's house (come bearing pizza at midnight) to see if anything is going on. Make it a rule that when he is not participating in sports activities or school, he is required to always answer his cell phone. That way you can call him periodically and hear if he sounds normal or not. Know the signs and symptoms of drug use (see the appendix), and give your son random drug tests if you suspect he's using. (You can buy test kits at your local pharmacy or order them over the Internet.) As a parent it's your job to know what at-risk behaviors to look for and to address them without apology—always keeping the goal of *connecting* to your son at the forefront of your mind.

ESTABLISH CLEAR CONSEQUENCES. Consequences for drug and/or alcohol use should be clearly communicated long before the behavior occurs. If your son chooses to drink or use, then it's your job to hold him accountable to the consequences. Jake's parents had begun telling him in middle school that his life was about choices on a daily basis. His choices would reveal his character and determine who he was and was to be. They stated clearly that if he drank alcohol he would lose (in the following order): social time with friends and girlfriends, driving privileges, sports activities, and all spending money from Mom and Dad.

When Jake was eighteen, I asked him what he thought of his parents laying it all out for him. "You know," he said, "they had always talked to me and my sisters about the dangers of even experimenting with drugs and especially alcohol, so it just didn't feel like I should do it. And then I went to the high school parties and saw how my buddies were acting like a bunch of lunatics and getting into so much trouble, and the whole scene just seemed like a waste of time." I asked him if his parents' approach made him want to disconnect from them, and he said, "Quite the opposite . . . we actually have a close, open relationship, which makes my friends really jealous." Communicating with your child about consequences for drug or alcohol use cannot begin too early. Far better to be proactive rather than retroactive.

I am a big advocate for tying consequences for substance use directly to driving privileges. Driving is critical to a young man's social life. Also, teens feel invincible, and most will attempt to drive even when they're under the influence because they feel like they can handle it. If they hurt someone, the liability for their choice will fall directly on you and your finances. I know a father who was sued because his son was driving while smoking pot and struck a minivan, killing a pregnant mother. Driving is a privilege, not a right, for a teenager. If your son is not yet in the driving years, you can require drug/alcohol education as a consequence of his using. You can find this through a local counselor or treatment facility, or you and your son can go online and find educational resources.

EMPOWER YOUR SON. Set up safe opportunities (when your son is not in trouble) to talk and process appropriate choices that allow him to feel like he still has some control and power in his life. Nathan, age sixteen, used to party weekly—sometimes three and four times a week. His parents enrolled him in an inpatient rehabilitation program for six months because his alcohol consumption was out of control. As the aftercare provider for this family, my primary goal was to have them talk and listen to each other in a safe environment.

They agreed to weekly roundtable discussions. Prior to the first roundtable the family came up with their "safe house" contract, which encouraged everyone to discuss openly, without judgment, how they were doing. After three months of participating according to the safe house rules, Nathan told me he was starting to feel closer to his family and more in control of his life within parental guidelines. Two years later Nathan is still sober and connected more than ever to his parents.

Three Choices

In the face of your son using drugs or alcohol, you have three choices:

1. **LET IT RIDE.** Wait until he's eighteen and then wish him well. This will send a pretty loud message that you don't like him enough to fight for him to like himself. One of the pioneers of modern psychiatry said years ago that as damaging as physical and sexual abuse is to a child, *far more damaging* is growing up in a home where he or she is neglected. When you think about it, that is an astounding statement. Staying tuned in to our sons and showing them that we like them can be hard work, but it's well worth the effort if capturing our sons' hearts is what we're after.

2. **BE INCONSISTENT.** This is where most parents of kids who are acting out end up: They pursue them sometimes and give up other times. I urge you to either make a choice to pursue or not. Parents who go back and forth actually make things worse for kids. Adolescents want (whether they admit it or not) safety and consistency. When it's confusing to figure out what's coming next, a lot of kids adopt the attitude, "What the heck, I might as well do whatever is right in front of me right now and hope it's not a big deal this time."

3. **FIGHT FOR YOUR SON.** Let him know you know what's going on, that you may have blown it with him in the past, that you're not always good at this parenting

thing, but you're not giving up. There is *effort* involved in connecting, and you must be willing to do most of the work initially. Too many parents try to connect one or two times and then drop out when their kid shuts them down. Believe it or not, your son may just be getting warmed up, especially if you've not been connecting for a while. How many years have you *not* talked about what's going on at school, not asked about his favorite music or movies, not been curious about how his friends are doing (not just what bad behavior they are up to)? Believe me: Boys *want* to talk about their lives. They are looking for someone who will keep pursuing them.

I recently climbed Mount Rainier, in Washington state. I had sixty-five pounds of gear on my back. It was heavy, and we were slogging through thigh-deep snow a good part of the climb. I had an objective, a goal—to stand on top of that mountain. Was it fun? Mountaineering in general is not fun; it is a ton of work. But while I'm in the process of working my way toward a summit, I enjoy the majesty of something so much bigger than myself and the problems of the moment. There is magic and majesty in the midst of exhausting work.

That's how parenting a boy is. Look for magic—moments when you connect. Look for majesty—when he gets it and no longer believes that getting high is worth feeling low. And remember that this is about something bigger than you and the problems your son is facing right now. This is about your son's heart finding roots in your love, allowing him to find his own wings and fly.

Bottom line: The best antidote to teenagers using drugs and alcohol is not just parental involvement; it is parents who *like* their kids. I hope this chapter has challenged you to *choose your son* and let him know that you are doing so because you like him! If this is your attitude, then *the chase is on.*

GO FOR IT!

ON YOUR MARKS!

Sit down with your family and come up with your own "safe house" contract. In a nonthreatening way explain to your kids your goal of a drug- and alcohol-free home, and open the dialogue with them by saying you want to hear what they see and experience regarding substance abuse at school, youth group, the soccer field, etc. Have in mind a few specific rules that you want to incorporate in the family contract, but in this exercise really listen to your kids and let them dictate what they want so they are taking ownership of the contract.

GET SET!

Spend some time creating a communication "key" for yourself. This would be your personal cheat sheet to keep you stay focused on open communication with your teen. As your son shares information with you about what he is seeing or hearing about substances invading his friends' or his world, you will have some appropriate responses ready. For example, "I am so thankful that you shared that with me" or "I appreciate your trusting me with that." These kinds of responses will keep communication open.

GO!

Make yourself uncomfortable! Educate and acculturate yourself on what is really out there in the teen world. Rent some teen movies, including the ones about drugs and alcohol. Listen to teen music when you are by yourself on the way to pick up your son from a friend's house. This will help you empathize with how hard he has it with the constant bombardment of pressure. Then surprise him by telling him you read the bio on his favorite band member or saw the latest teen buzz movie. I promise he will look at you as if he has never seen you before, but you will have captivated his interest, and you, in turn, may like him more!

6

When the Cork Blows

April 20, 1999, is a day in my community that will never be forgotten. *Columbine.* In the words of a local reporter, "Anger visited our community." Anger took the lives of innocent people and traumatized thousands of others all across the country. So much so that a survey conducted three years later of kids ages eleven to seventeen found that 40 percent feared being shot or otherwise harmed by a peer at school.[4] I am still counseling a small handful of young people who were victimized on that day.

So why did it happen? Many have tried to figure that out, but few have found real answers. In the last twenty years youth worldwide are acting out at a level that is progressively more aggressive. When I was in high school, kids acted out their anger by getting into a fistfight or throwing a chair. Today kids bring guns and knives to school and use them.

Before we throw our arms up in complete exasperation at their aggressive behavior, let's realize that boys have been given permission to act out. Actors, athletes, musicians, disgruntled employees, and even fellow students are in the news regularly acting out their anger. Unfortunately, like a steady IV drip, teens are fed by their culture that anger is *the* way for boys to express emotion.

Dads, this is a good time for you to examine how *you* were raised and, again, what you think it means to be a man. For more boys than most would imagine, being a man means "ratcheting it up." One father told me about his childhood years, with very little emotion: "My dad had good aim. But sometimes he got a little out of control and the stick would land on my back. There were no broken bones, though. No scars. Especially from the verbal assaults of being called stupid, lazy, and worthless." What are you teaching your son about anger and what it means to be a man? In his excellent book *I Don't Want to Talk About It*, Terrence Real summarizes why this question is vital in beginning to look at anger in adolescent boys: "And so the chain goes, across generations, link to link. Whether he knew it or not, my father was doing more than meting out punishment for imagined infractions [or treating my mom with disrespect for her failings]. He was teaching me, just as he had been taught, what it means to be a man."[5]

Moms, if you don't understand your son's anger, understand that permission to act out flows in stages and steps. For example, you're in a relationship and your boyfriend or spouse acts out by raising his voice at you. If you choose not to respond or react to how you were disrespected then, you give away a little bit of your power to stand up for yourself and require respect. You give him permission to yell. A natural progression of unchecked aggression in a boy goes, in general, in the following order:

1. Raised voice/yelling/foul language
2. Breaking of objects/destruction of property
3. Possibly injury to an animal
4. Physical aggression, which may result in bodily injury or even murder

If you are unable to shut down the beginning of disrespect you will have a really hard time shutting it down as your son progresses in the above skills. Skills? Yes, I said skills! A young man learns that he can and will gain power and control by being out of control. In a teenager's mind he sees that acting out gives him something in return, so he is tricked into thinking that acting out is a skill. Of course it's not really a skill, but a reaction to a variety of emotions that a boy learns no other way to handle. Some young men will succeed at honing this behavior into a razor-edged weapon.

Two years ago I had a teenager in my office who was beyond angry with me. I had confronted him about his positive drug test and told him straight up that he was not pulling his weight at home or school or following the conditions of his probation following his arrest for possession of crystal methamphetamine. I had already reported him to his probation officer for having used again. Chris and I had forged a good relationship over several weeks, and he had been calling me daily to check in and give me an update on his sobriety or lack thereof. He really wanted help with his addiction.

While we were conversing Chris was gliding a three-inch knife into the grooves in the wood of the armchair in my office. After I repeatedly requested that he put the knife away, his anger escalated, and he hurled the knife at me from eight feet away. My first reaction was shock. I saw the knife coming right at me and I instinctively put up my hands in a defensive pose — which I'm glad I did or the knife would have lodged itself in my chest. Instead the blade cut me across my hand and upper torso.

Now, looking back, I'm glad I didn't jump up and attempt to restrain him. I simply got out of my chair, grabbed my cell phone off my desk, and called 911. The police who work across the street from me were at my door in less than ninety seconds and arrested Chris on attempted first-degree assault. Right before he was led out of my office, I told him I loved him and that I would see him soon.

Chris spent ten days in jail while his probation was revoked and reinstated. When the assistant district attorney contacted me in regard to being a victim in the aggravated assault case, I told her I wanted to continue working with Chris and maintain my professional relationship. After a long silence she told me I was crazy, but the courts soon gave me clearance to be Chris's primary provider for ongoing treatment.

When Chris came back for his next session, we talked about his pattern of aggression. When he felt backed up against a wall, his "problem-solving technique" was to use intimidation, explosive verbal assaults, and even physical violence. I told him I had three options:

1. I could call the police or his probation officer every time he acted out in any way, and they could haul him back to jail.
2. I could kick him out of my office then and there, wish

him the best, and recommend to his parents that *they* call the cops anytime he violated his probation or blew his top.

3. He and I could spend some time getting to the truth—the emotions and experiences that provoked his anger. I told him that I was going to make him a one-time offer: a chance at 100 percent truth and 100 percent grace. He began to do the hard work to understand himself, because in the extreme moment of his extreme anger when he threw the knife at me, he learned I didn't hate his anger and that made him wonder if maybe I might be one person who didn't hate him. It was worth a shot.

Chris continued in treatment for eleven more months and was successfully discharged from my program and from probation. He has held down a job, attends college classes, has a steady girlfriend, and has reconciled with his parents. In choosing to climb toward the goal of being connected to others, he has kept me in the loop of his life and often solicits my counsel as he continues to learn how to appropriately communicate his thoughts and feelings. He has not assaulted anyone physically or verbally in over a year.

Boys Will Be Boys?

The ball of feelings that result in anger comes from the experience of normal human emotions. Teenagers have not grown enough of a brain to separate out and process all of those emotions. A common result is that they wind everything up into one big ball (like those balls of rubber bands boys love to make when they're bored), and just let it fly!

One reason we let boys get away with inappropriate disrespect and aggressive behavior is that we buy into that all-too-often-used adage "Boys will be boys." When we allow our sons to justify their reactions to what is happening around them, they don't learn what else to do with the emotions of frustration, boredom, humiliation, injustice, etc. Boys become hardwired to be angry because they trace ruts in their brains that the only way to respond to psychic distress is to explode.

Kids are educated very early as to what is acceptable and what is not. The etiology of teenage aggression can start as early as infancy—it is progressive, learned behavior. Unresolved conflict, miscommunication, and expectations that are unfair, unrealistic, or unspoken are just a few of the things boys use to justify negative behaviors that are often tolerated when they should be confronted. It's easy to want to look the other way in the early stages of progressive aggression. After all, boys will be boys. But little boys who are allowed to be inappropriately aggressive with no consequences begin to trace a path in their brains that aggressive action is what it means to be alive and be a guy.

My oldest son is "Mr. Excitement." One night when I came home from work, I asked everyone if they wanted to go out for pizza. My son was so excited that he bit me on the thigh and left a nice reminder of my dinner invitation for a week! That wasn't the first time my wife and I found ourselves frustrated that we were not impacting our son enough to have him check his impulses. In many situations we were tempted to ignore his aggressive energy or give in to his persistence. We found that we were tired and withdrawing, and our positive energy toward him was waning. However, I knew in the back of my mind what he might look like ten years from now—having an impulsivity that wouldn't self-regulate or respond to the feelings of others.

In this early phase of parenting, my wife and I have to be on our toes in order to be one step in front of our son while paying attention to his developmental growth, language, and behavioral skills. After several instances of watching his energy target us or his siblings with hostile behavior (which didn't involve any more biting, but did include hitting his sister in the head with a hockey stick!), we decided we needed a change of rules. We started by incorporating more personal time for him. We have special times with each of our children called "mommy time" or "daddy time," but he needed more than the structure we had in place. We also decided we would be more physical in giving hugs when we saw his frustration building. We found special ways to point out and reward positive behavior. Most important, we became more cognizant of how we were internally reacting to him, which, of course, influenced how he was reacting to us. We practiced a lot more of joining him where he was. His response has been remarkable. He softens more quickly, deescalates, and becomes a lot more open to our direction. The results were not immediate, but they came and continue to come in ways we could not have foreseen.

The Perfect Storm

Researchers have found that young boys who are angry are cuddled less and that older boys are encouraged less when they are expressing anger. If this is true, then we are culpable in positioning the "cork to blow." We are teaching boys that when they are angry they are not lovable or worth dealing with. Actually, I have found that anger is the *perfect storm* in which we can give love, respect, support, and effective guidance to our boys.

Rich, age nineteen, is a wonderful communicator and has a tremendous heart. After working hard in therapy for over a year, he had earned a place on one of my "2xtreme Dream" teams. As a reward for intensive and successful personal growth, some of my clients are given the opportunity to go on a "dream trip." The youth have seven challenges they must meet in order to receive the reward:

1. Create a treatment plan and program that reflects positive growth and change
2. Maintain appropriate academic standards
3. Maintain a sober lifestyle (no drugs or alcohol whatsoever)
4. Actively participate in resolving conflict in the home
5. Have no negative police contact
6. Create and participate in a community service project
7. Maintain a part-time job or participate in an after-school program (sports, clubs, etc.)

If after a year of "training" in the above standards a youth does not have three strikes on his record, then he will receive his dream. Through the years I have taken my guys, along with a small adult support team, on adventures to Disney World in Florida, Mount Kilimanjaro in Africa, the high Andes of Peru, and Europe's tallest mountain, which is in southern Russia.

Rich and I had developed a strong bond and a wonderful relationship during his training for his 2xtreme Dream, which would involve climbing one of the highest peaks in South America. Before he could fulfill all that his dream entailed, however, he decided to drink alcohol, which, of course, is against team policy. He was confronted and told that his trip was over and that he was to return home with me.

Rich and another team member who had blown his contract accompanied me on a twenty-hour bus ride just to get to the main terminal in Lima, Peru. From there we still had an hour's taxi ride to the airport. Rich, who had not said a word since we got on the bus, pulled me aside in the terminal and told me that he was not returning to the States with me. He was angry that he had made a bad choice and was having a hard time following through with his consequence. He wanted me to rescue him and say it was okay and that I would give him another chance. I did not. I wanted Rich to have to sit downwind of himself and experience what the consequences of his bad choices smelled like.

He was furious. He said, "I want you to tell me that you love me, support me, and that everything between us is going to be all right!" My internal response was *What? You want love, support, and everything to be okay? You blew it, brother, and you deserve this consequence.* I didn't actually say any of that. What I did say was, "I do love you, I do not support your poor decision, and your choices will affect our relationship until you are ready to assume some personal responsibility. You also are no longer part of the team and will not be financially supported."

I turned and got into a taxi with my other client. My heart hurt! On one level I was shocked that Rich would not comply and face the immediate consequence of losing his dream, but on another level I understood that despite all the work he'd done in therapy, he still needed to buck the system. He still didn't know what to do with all his emotion other than make a very stupid decision, get mad, and sabotage himself. When I left him standing in the bus depot to deal with all his feelings as well as the consequences of staying behind, I believed the experience would prompt some serious personal growth. I loved him enough to leave him, to instruct him through my behavior that he needed to assume responsibility rather than try to pin his fury and disappointment on me. I called Rich's parents from the airport, and they supported my decision to fly home without their son. At age nineteen, with no international travel experience and less than $250 in his pocket, Rich had to figure out—with his parents' help—how to get home from South America on his own.

A few days after he returned to the States, Rich contacted me, wanting to start a reconciliation process. When we got together, we stood in the parking lot of my office for over an hour, and I told him his behavior was unacceptable but that I did love him despite not approving of his separating himself from me in an act of rebellion and anger. He was sincerely apologetic and expressed gratitude that I was still willing to offer him grace after the mistake he'd made. We repaired our relationship and Rich finished his treatment program with me three months later.

Soon after that I saw Rich with a group of his friends and one friend was acting out aggressively. I watched Rich model what I modeled to him. He said to his friend, "Man, I know you're mad about stuff, but you can't act that way here. You need to leave until you get yourself under control. Call me, and we'll get together later." That's the greatest gift a parent or counselor can receive—seeing a young man model to others what you've modeled to him.

A Crash Course in Crashing Boys

Anger is everywhere and in everyone. Some choose to problem-solve their frustrations and circumstances and find success in conveying and communicating their heart rather than breaking someone else's with inappropriate reactions. But it seems that this is the exception rather than the rule among teenage boys.

Brad, age sixteen, acted out in any area he could. He was on probation for theft, assault, and possession of an illegal substance. As I got to know him, he would regularly raise his voice toward me and grab me in an aggressive way. Each time he did, I would look at him and ask why I was the target for his internal rage. Brad, unfortunately, never had a good reason, just a guess: stress at home, school, girlfriend, or athletic demands. I responded by telling him he had great excuses but no real reasons. In other words, his emotions were valid, but he was not doing the work to determine the source of his anger.

Halfway through his work with me he told me he thought he was addicted to acting out his anger. Brad said it best: "It is the only time I really feel alive." It also relieved him of all those roiling emotions. Even though it left everyone else bloody and battered, Brad felt better.

I ask many moms in my counseling office if they would be all right knowing that their son is verbally abusive to his girlfriend. The answer is always, "No way!" I will also ask a young man who is verbally aggressive with his mother whether he would come back for another session with me if I spoke to his mother with the same obscenities that he hurls at her. His response is as you might imagine: "That's my mom, dude. You can't talk like that to her." So I ask, "Why is it acceptable for you but not for me?" By asking these questions, I can help him see — without a lot of unproductive shame — that he is dehumanizing himself when he talks to others — especially females — disrespectfully.

One of my client's moms had a discussion with her son about why the "F" word is not appropriate. Kids really think it is, because they hear it about three hundred times a day. She explained that it violated her, and she asked that he not say it, out of respect for her. She asked him to find other ways to communicate his anger *to her*. However, on the day a friend backed into his new (to him) car and totaled it, she said, "Son, rage on! Sometimes extreme words are appropriate for extreme situations."

Now, you might not agree with this mom, but the principle is that she was teaching her son that she was not afraid of his anger, which enabled him to respect her. When you are *with* your son when he is angry, you are telling him that you can handle his anger, and gradually he will be able to acknowledge that the angry behavior is a reaction to not getting his way, feeling like he is losing power, or not knowing what to do with a host of emotions.

Sometimes you'll need to shut your son down in the moment, but not shut him off. In my experience we react to anger by trying to swoop in and save the day or dismiss it or ignore it entirely, making our sons feel like wimps or fools. We do that especially with anger because we just hate it and don't know how to deal with it. Let me suggest a few approaches you might not have tried before.

DON'T TELL YOUR SON TO CALM DOWN. That is not a good problem-solving technique. You may know that because it's likely your son has told *you* to calm down a few times, and you found yourself becoming more defensive. In my adolescence, when I was angry and acting out, if someone told me to count to ten so that I could calm down, I would spend ten seconds thinking of ways I could act out.

DON'T ASK YOUR SON WHAT HE'S FEELING. Often teenagers live on the edge on their emotions and don't know what they feel. Change one word. Really. Just move from "What are you feeling?" to "What are you thinking?" If your son is acting out—particularly with anger—ask him what he's *thinking*. If you don't know what he's thinking, never guess what he's feeling. You may think you know (especially moms), but don't waste time going back and forth to his bedroom to say, "I know what you're feeling." He doesn't want to talk about what he's feeling, but what he's thinking. This approach may be counterintuitive for moms and some dads, but eventually the floodgates will open and their sons will start talking. There will be lots of free association that seems like a bunch of disconnected thoughts that don't have anything to do with the anger. Don't analyze, don't evaluate. Just get your son talking. That's when connection becomes possible.

I went bouldering with a client not too long ago. I have a policy to not go higher than ten feet without a crash pad. This kid was fifteen years old and a risk-taker. Before I knew it, he had climbed up forty feet, and I didn't feel safe with it. I explained what would happen if he slipped and fell. He responded, "Here you are being my mother."

I quickly replied, "I'm not your mother, and I'm not telling you to come down. I'm telling you what the consequences would be. Now, you tell me what happens if you fall."

He said, "Well, I could break my ankle, hit my skull, and die. And my parents would probably sue you!" After two more moves he started coming down. Watching him, I was reminded that what makes sense to a kid often does not make sense to an adult. As parents, we often serve our son best not by getting in his face and trying to prove something to him, but by allowing him to participate in thinking through his actions and their consequences.

Recently, my ever-adventurous eldest son was climbing a ladder too high for him. I asked him, "What might happen if you keep climbing?" Much like my fifteen-year-old client, he thought it through. He said, "I could fall and crack my head open."

"Then what?" I asked. He answered, "I might have to go to the hospital. That wouldn't be fun." He kept climbing. I kept encouraging him to think it through. If I said, "Don't do that! You could kill yourself; get down!" he would obey, but there might be disconnection between us. While I was there to make sure he was safe, I was teaching him to think things through. I was allowing him to be a boy. I asked again, "How do you think your mom, sister, brothers, and I would feel if you cracked your head open?" He thought again. He took two steps down the ladder. I could have pulled him off that ladder and been done with it. I could have "won," but I didn't have anything to prove.

DON'T PERSONALIZE YOUR SON'S ANGER. When a boy is angry, let him feel his feelings. That doesn't mean you let him disrespect you. Just let him know that you know he's angry. Show up. Be present to his emotion, simply by acknowledging it. He doesn't need you to be in his face; he needs to know that you *hear* his anger. Don't assert your own agenda. Guys need to process it out.

Not personalizing our kids' emotions or offenses allows us as parents to really connect with them. The first time you tell your son "Thank you for sharing that with me," and don't overreact, or you take some time to process how you should respond, you will be sending the message that you are not judging him and you want him to tell you more.

One of my friends told me about her son's coming home from school early without permission. He was furious. He had worked hard on a project and been given a low grade. She wanted to swoop in and save the day, call the teacher, and tell him how hard her son had worked and how much he deserved a good grade. She would have totally emasculated him, mostly because she just didn't want him to be so mad. His hostility made her uncomfortable. His dad wisely let him vent, then advised him to return to school, express his anger, tell his teacher how hard he worked, and ask if there was room for negotiation on the grade. The teacher respected the boy's honest expression of anger and his willingness to come back and work things out. He gave him a slightly better grade. But far more important than the raised grade was the boy's raised self-esteem.

We're All in This Together

When you were in middle school, did you take an anger management class? Did you take a personal communication class in college? Did you take a course in how to stay connected to your son? No. That's why it's so hard to know how to communicate. We have little training and few positive role models.

Parenting is tough, and it's always a work in progress. If you're committed, however, then you can be successful in communicating: "I don't always know how to do it right, but I'm not going to give up on trying to be connected to you. Anger will take up all the space in the room so there is no room for connection. So I'm not going to pretend it's no big deal when I'm angry or when you are."

Recently, one of my sons was jabbering away telling me all about his day. I was tired, distracted, and thinking about a dozen other things. I was "uh-huhing" him. In that moment he grabbed my face and said, "Daddy, I'm trying to com-*mun*-i-cate." I was reminded that kids lose hope quickly. If your son has lost hope that he can grab your face and get your attention, then start taking small steps again. If you learn to do the little things well—confess your failures, ask questions that express genuine interest in him, disclose your own struggles with anger or reacting to anger—then you can do the big things well, like turning around an aggressive, angry teenage boy. Whenever you can engage your son with nothing to prove, then *the chase is on.*

GO FOR IT!

ON YOUR MARKS!

Have a conversation with your son when there is some emotional balance in both of your worlds. Write out five things you can do to deescalate a situation that looks like it may fly out of control. Also ask your son to create his own "hot list" of things he could do to deescalate, such as playing a video game, hitting his punching bag, doing fifty push-ups, taking a walk, or listening to his music. Ask him to suggest three things that you as his mom or dad could do to help him when he feels like he may blow his lid. For example, asking him calmly when things start to heat up, "Should we take a break?"

GET SET!

Establish some fair and reasonable expectations that you both will keep in mind during conflict. These "rules of engagement" might include the following: no foul language, no problem solving for the other person or projecting what you think he should do when he is frustrated, no blaming.

GO!

Set up a weekly check-and-balance time to evaluate how you are doing at being present to each other during conflict and abiding by your established rules. Always be willing to reevaluate if your contract needs to be changed for the benefit of each other and your ultimate success at staying connected.

7

Sex Is Everything

About five years ago I did some research for a parenting seminar I was teaching about teenage sex, statistics, and habits. I simply typed "teenage sex statistics" into my search engine and was plunged into a labyrinth of pornographic websites that highlighted teens who have sex. I tried to close out the pornographic sites, but more and more appeared on the screen. Dumbfounded by this black hole of pornography, I documented how many porn sites I had to close to get back to my original request. Seventy-eight.

I should not have been surprised. After all, I know something far more compelling than Internet sites. I know stories.

Bryce, age fifteen, is addicted to pornography. He was introduced to this dark and cryptic world by his older brother when he was twelve years old. Bryce's parents sent him to me after catching him using their credit card to enter pornographic websites. When they discovered that Bryce had racked up *twenty-four thousand dollars* in site charges, his parents were quickly educated. They had had no idea that he was spending so much time online in the dark corridors of porn sites. He cruised chat rooms and called 900 numbers and the local "connection" line, where for $1.95 to $4.95 per minute, he could have a live conversation with someone about anything—including getting an anonymous woman to whisper sweet nothings in his ear while he masturbated. All of these activities fueled his deep desire to connect, but left him in the vicious cycle of feeling even emptier and longing for relationship more intensely as he fed an out-of-control fantasy life.

Though it may sound extreme to most parents, I tell Bryce's story right away to say that boys who act out sexually on an extreme scale reveal what is true of most young men when it comes to their sexuality. They are not just sex machines, eager to get, use, and discard girls. Rather, they are boys longing for connection and life in a culture that has taught them that the way a man connects is to have sex, be sexual, and act cavalierly about it afterward, even if he feels guilty, ashamed, and alone. In her book about teenage girls and sex, *"Mom, Sex Is No Big Deal!"*, author Sharon Hersh explains that every boy has a story: "The sex-is-no-big deal mantra has resulted in men and women carelessly and thoughtlessly violating one another and themselves. When we all laugh at Joey on *Friends*, we send a message to boys and girls about sex that isn't the least bit funny."[6]

Kyle is another example of a boy we might consider disgusting if we didn't see beyond his behavior to his heart. Kyle got into posting messages on Internet links, just to find someone with whom he could play sensual games. At age seventeen he craved connection and spent $700 to try to get it. He got caught using his dad's credit card and using his dad's and grandmother's personal computers to satiate his desires.

Teenage boys may seem oblivious to consequences or clueless about their extreme behaviors, but Kyle got it. Most boys do. He told me, "The one thing I wanted was to have someone interested in me. But I was walking around in this huge lie while sabotaging the one true thing I wanted." At some level teenagers feel uncomfortable in their own skin. Because they feel like their every move is being judged, watched, and analyzed, anxiety becomes part of their walk, and then they are vulnerable to the invitation offered to them at every turn—on television, in movies, and in music videos; the invitation to feel okay in your own skin by acting out sexually is issued to them continuously.

Author and sociologist Robert Shaw says it brilliantly in his book, *The Epidemic*: "Teenagers are like lobsters in their molting season. They are tender. *They do not know how to be in the world* [emphasis added]. They cast about for guidelines. If they don't find them at home, they can be easily pushed and seduced by peers."[7] (And, I would add, gobbled up by predators far and wide.)

The Sexual Behaviors of Teenage Boys

This is the area that parents are most blindsided in because it takes place behind closed doors and grows in the secret fantasies of the mind. In high school, boys are entering into a new world, but many are already bombarded by sex from the media culture and their peers. Freshmen boys are all about adventure and survival and quickly see as they enter the doors of high school that relationships between the sexes are the key to fitting in. Many of my young high school clients tell me that one of their goals is to have sex before graduating from high school. That's just part of the adventure.

What they quickly learn is that woven within this "adventure" is the survival of dealing with what goes on behind the scenes — of being harassed and mocked for sexual inexperience and naïveté, being heartbroken by girls who lead them on and dump them, and feeling guilty about doing things they really didn't want to do. Sharon Hersh writes, "It's important to note that according to a 2003 *Seventeen* magazine survey, 33 percent of boys who engaged in sexual intercourse felt pressure from *girls* to do so."[8]

A boy's sexual development begins in earnest *before* high school. In middle school today there is lots of "fooling around." When I was in high school, I knew a *few* kids who were having sex. In middle school today *many* kids engage in oral sex. In fact several TV news magazine programs have shocked parents with the reality of middle school oral sex parties. Middle school kids also engage in anal sex because they don't want to "lose their virginity." Before we scoff at their ignorance, we need to ask how many conversations have we had with our middle school boys about oral and anal sex. And we need to remember that these are boys whose brains have not yet caught up with their bodies. They are in a culture that puts them at risk for sexual foolishness, setting them up for experimenting with sexual behavior in high school.

I have found in talking with many hundreds of teenage boys that they go through a predictable process of exploring their sexuality during the high school years. Let's consider a typical freshman boy who enters a large high school in metro Denver. At fourteen, with acne on his face and braces on his teeth, he faces two thousand other students. As he walks through the halls, he's wondering, *What am I supposed to do?* He has antennas on his head; he's bumping into things, and, tragically, what he bumps into from day one is conversations about who "hooked up" over the weekend, stories about boys getting "blow jobs" in the bathroom at school, and challenges thrown out as to when he is going to "score."

During his sophomore year he begins building a chosen group that he is going to hang out with. He decides who he's going to be as he gets coaching from peers who are just as lost as he is. He realizes there are other ideologies about sex than those he's heard from his family, and the encouragement to "go for it" is intriguing to a naturally adventurous boy longing to belong in an ever-expanding world that threatens to swallow him up. Next come the opportunities to choose new ways of thinking about sex and to participate, which *most* teen boys do. There is a lot of sexual acting out during this year, as boys foolishly believe they are wise enough to make decisions about sex.

On a dare one of my sophomore clients received oral sex in the chemistry lab while the teacher was lecturing. Another sophomore had sex in the high school bathroom while everyone was in class. Another had sex during the church youth group meeting. While everyone was singing and watching a skit, he and one of the girls snuck out the back and went to his car. This was not uncommon; other kids were doing it as well. I have found that parents are incredibly naive about kids who are acting out—especially *their* kids. Kids are having a lot of sex, a lot of unprotected sex, in a lot of unprotected environments. According to a 2005 report from the Centers for Disease Control, 47 percent of high school students have had sexual intercourse, 14 percent have had four or more partners, and 34 percent of the sexually active teens did not use a condom during their last sexual experience.[9] Because many youths do not report their activities honestly on surveys, I believe these statistics are *low* compared to the reality of high school kids' sexual practices today.

During their junior year of high school, boys begin trying to elevate themselves within their chosen group. "Encouragement" comes from others guys with weak egos (pretty typical for developing teenage boys), suggesting that if they act out they will get attention—and *attention feels like self-esteem to a teenage boy.* Consider a girl who loses twenty pounds; everyone says, "You look great," but this often only encourages her to lose more—even to the point of becoming broomstick-thin and even sick. For the guy, when he hears, "I can't believe you scored," it often encourages him to score with more, to the point where he feels really bad about himself and his behaviors.

During a boy's senior year of high school, there is a type of "closure." Guys make big decisions here as to whether they are going to continue on the sexual path they've chosen in high school. There is an introspective look at life, because most guys do feel bad about the path of carnage they've created, and they realize they really do want to sustain mutual relationships. Many boys I see in this stage have learned that sexually acting out will not get them there. They have regrets. With the right coaching they begin to realize they can create something new as they enter into the next phase of life, but guys who don't have someone to talk to about this (and most do not) will continue on the same path. And I don't think I need to say much about the scary sexual climate in college today. Statistics show that the number of young men who are sexually active in college increases by more than 30 percent from those who are sexually active in high school.[10]

Kids Lie About Sex

Parents need to know that kids lie about having sex. Lying is about guilt. They will look you in the eye and lie. They don't want you to feel low about their choices—as low as they feel about themselves. Guys spend so much time telling themselves that they are doing the right thing when they know in their heart they are not. I believe that God has kindly woven into the fabric of every soul something that will not be satisfied with untruth. Teenage boys are not satisfied with just adding another notch to their belt. The unspoken internal struggle often leads to anger and self-medicating, which leads to justification of their choices. Boys fall into a hole of disassociation from themselves and disconnection from their hearts as they do things that take them further and further from their goal—connecting and feeling loved, not just hooking up.

Adolescents know intuitively that they shouldn't have sex, but the pressure to perform and keep up with what everyone else is doing is a powerful tempter. Once they give in, they believe they cannot return, because they find out about the power of sex, and sex then becomes the power in their lives.

Adam, age seventeen, was not a real troublemaker. He went to a summer party and had sex with a girl he had never met before because she approached him during the first five minutes of the party and told him she would be waiting upstairs to have sex with him. (Remember, I told you earlier about the survey that says one-third of all guys feel pressure from girls to have sex.) That type of assertive behavior only fed Adam's desire for fantasy, which then had to be fed again and again. The assertiveness also fed his desire to connect, and sex was the link to connection for that night. It was free and easy.

Adam came to me for his session the following day and told me his story. After a few questions he told me he felt bad about his choice and really did not feel like he connected with this girl. He admitted, "It was just sex." Adam was a Christian and wanted to live by his convictions to be pure. He felt like that one night had tainted him forever. He already felt hooked in the "What difference does it make now?" mentality.

Boys lie to their parents because they know their choices will not be met with approval, and they do not want to get caught up in their parents' moralizing and lecturing. Likewise, they believe the lie that their friends and the media tell them: that *sex is connection*. Because so many teenage girls have bought into this lie as well and are willing to be an "outlet" for boys' sexual expression, *both* boys and girls suffer the consequences.

Pleasure Seeking

We quickly recognize that girls are used and discarded and heartbroken because they've believed some boy who told them they would be together forever if they had sex. But there is tragedy for boys as well, and I am passionate that we understand this so we don't buy into the mentality that sex is really not a big deal for teenage boys. As I said in the previous chapter, "Boys will be boys" is one of the most damaging, stereotypical descriptors we have for adolescent guys, because in essence it gives them permission to "go ahead, get it out of your system." As we've already discussed, the real tragedy is that it often takes over their system.

As I get to the heart of what has happened to the adolescent male culture with regard to sex, I need to tell you a few more stories. They may seem extreme, but I urge you not to look for differences between these boys and your son, but to look for similarities and to wonder if you really know what is happening with your son.

Jared, age sixteen, set some academic, athletic, and relationship goals in the first week of school. As he shared these with me, we seemed to be having a normal goal-setting session until he blurted out that he had a sexual goal as well. "Oh?" I said. Jared proceeded to tell me that he wanted to have sex with thirty-seven different girls this school year. One girl per week. I had to force my mouth closed before I said, "You're joking, right?" I wanted to jump up and slap him!

Jared, like almost every teenager I have encountered, defined a part of his identity by his sexual activity. Relationships with teens of the opposite sex are defined by a common vocabulary. If you've never heard of the terms *hooking up*, *friends with benefits*, and *f-ing partners*, then I encourage you to talk with your son and ask him to define them for you. There is no real emotional or relational component to these definitions. Guys champion each other to go for it. But please recall what I said earlier: Teenage boys are not sex fiends. Their insecurity and need to belong drives their desire to have sex.

No matter what question I threw Jared's way in response to his goal of having sex with thirty-seven girls his junior year, he combated my efforts by telling me "I'm gonna do this." Jared was not totally "successful" in his quest; however, twenty-five girls did fall to his seduction. In the end even some of his friends were telling him that he was really messed up. He still checks in with me periodically. I think he is living a remorseful life, but he is not able to verbalize it or do anything about it.

I asked him once, "What do you really get out of sex?" (When I ask this question, *everyone* looks at me with the same expression Jared did: *You mean you don't know?*) I said, "Seriously."

Jared answered, "It feels great."

I pressed. "I mean more on an emotional level—what are you getting out of it?" He, like most guys I counsel, couldn't answer. Some teens who have been working with me for a while may say it's drawing them closer to their partner in a relationship. I then ask, "Is that really appropriate for where you are with this girl?" This is a question I have to leave rhetorical—to allow my guys to struggle with who they are and who they want to be.

I have asked countless clients at all levels on the sexual continuum—from Jared-like sexual activity to heavy petting with a girl to an active fantasy life—the following question: "What does sex provide for you aside from an orgasm?" These are their answers:

- Sex is a time-filler.
- Sex provides me with acceptance socially; everyone else is doing it.
- Sex feels great, it's fun, and it allows me to feel a part of a group of kids.
- Sex is a great "excuse"—a justification accepted among my peers for not *really* connecting behaviorally or emotionally.

These answers may seem shallow, but it makes total sense to me that teens are walking around like human antennae, bumping into each other, thinking that this is how they are going to fit in and satisfy the craving in their souls.

So are you feeling overwhelmed? Hopeless? Don't give up yet. But before we get to the good news, we need to look the bad news square in the face and try to understand it. Part of grasping what is happening with boys today sexually means understanding a little bit about neurophysiology and the hypothalamus.

When Sex Becomes an Addiction

Sex triggers hormonal reactions in the hypothalamus, the pleasure center of the brain. I tell the guys I work with that the more they are rewarding the hypothalamus now, the harder it's going to be to maintain the same type of stimulus later. It's important to note that there is a chemical reward for the fantasy, for the orgasm, and for the pleasure before, during, and after sex. What is enough when you are fourteen will not be enough when you are eighteen, and that will not be enough when you are twenty-five, and that will not be enough when you are forty-five. The big lie to guys in today's culture is that sex and sexually acting out will define them as men. The more the brain is being tweaked, the harder it is to stay focused in a monogamous relationship, and a young man satiated in sexual acting out will feel the need for multiple sex partners. In the end it can destroy the opportunity for a committed, mutually satisfying relationship—one of the most important elements of becoming a man.

I encourage you to hang in there before you say, "Not my son." Sexual addiction among teens is not just about the need to have sex multiple times a day or all day long, but about how much room sex takes up in the brain. For too many young men, because of the sexually saturated culture and the easy access, sex takes on a life of its own. It is its own beast.

The statistics are compelling and cannot be ignored. In May of 2000, the National Coalition to Protect Children and Families surveyed five *Christian* college campuses to see how the next generation was doing with sexual purity:

- Forty-eight percent of males admitted to current porn use.
- Sixty-eight percent of males said they had intentionally viewed a sexually explicit website at the school.[11]

If this survey reports what was going on several years ago on Christian college campuses, then we can only imagine the rate of sexual addiction today among young men in society at large. It begins in early adolescence with desensitization to sex through media, entertainment, and friends. I heard a few *years* ago that every week there are seven thousand new porn sites dedicated to the strong sexual appetite. Imagine how rampant porn sites are now! It is not news that males are stimulated visually and what they see that is sexually stimulating is everywhere—from Mom's Victoria's Secret catalog to the new websites popping up daily. Middle school boys begin to use masturbation as a way to self-medicate their growing adolescent angst. High school boys believe that acting out sexually is relating.

It doesn't take long for boys to discover the neurochemical release we discussed earlier in this chapter, which feeds their acting out. Parents get confused, thinking that their teen's sexual behavior is just about having an orgasm. This is partially true, but it's also about fantasy and release. This powerful combination of repeated neurochemical stimulation triggers fantasy and further release, which can set the stage for addiction.

Stages of Addiction

SATURATION. Sex is everywhere and in everything we see. Driving on their local highway, men are tantalized by billboards advertising the local strip club. Surfing the information highway, they are bombarded with spam asking for their vote for who is sexier, Jennifer Aniston or Angelina Jolie. Magazines and books offer instruction on how to spice up the sex in the bedroom. Advertisements during television sports showcase young models with next to no clothes advertising juicy hamburgers. Considering that many teens today cite boredom as one of their biggest problems, it's not hard to understand how sex fills a void.

INTRIGUE. Because sex is everywhere, who wouldn't be intrigued? There is the initial spark of arousal, which is normal. The body naturally responds to sexual stimuli, but no one is teaching kids what to do with that. Most boys who are stimulated visually store all this stimuli in a database in the back of their brain that they pull from later—creating a fantasy life that fuels addiction.

EXPERIMENTATION. Like any addiction, sexual addiction is progressive, and it begins with experimentation. As a boy dabbles with masturbating to pornography, he may progress to acting out in other ways, via phone sex, cybersex, oral sex parties and orgies, to engaging multiple sex partners. One of my clients described the progression: "I felt like I fell into a trash can by accident and then the trash just kept getting piled on higher and higher until I couldn't get out." He was thirteen years old. If you don't think your son fits in one of the stories

I've told, I urge you to know what he's watching, where he's surfing, where the seeds of addiction are being planted. No guy is immune to sexual addiction.

COPING. This is morning-after guilt: "I won't do this again." But then you start thinking about the pleasure, the reward—so "just one more time. . . ." When parents catch their son using porn and/or masturbating, they often think he just wants relief. My experience with hundreds of boys has taught me that it's not just about the orgasm. It is about the whole cycle—fantasy, intensity, pleasure, guilt, and relief. This cycle is what guys get addicted to.

LIFESTYLE. Pornography and/or sexually acting out equals guilt initially, but once it becomes comfortable, it leads to indulgence, which ends in the tragic reality of a young man who has no significant attachment in a real relationship.

I spent three years counseling with Lance, who came to me at the age of twenty-six. He held a master's degree from UCLA and was making a six-figure income. He told me he was "living the dream"—cool car, great house, great vacations, long-term friendships, and a fiancée. The truth for him was that he was masturbating sometimes twenty times per day. He was not masturbating for the orgasm. He was trying to feel connected and alive. He loved his fantasy life and could not get out of it. Likewise, he could not be intimate with his fiancée, which is why he came to talk with me. Lance's lifestyle was the consequence of being hyperstimulated by porn and acting out sexually way too early. He could not walk away. And now he wanted to connect intimately and be successful in a monogamous lifestyle, but he couldn't.

He wept telling me his story. He wept because he was lonely and isolated and could not get the filth out of his brain. He felt like a robot. He had a schedule to keep or, like the Cookie Monster, he would freak out if he didn't get a fix. This all started at age twelve when his father introduced him to *Playboy* magazine. At fourteen he was caught masturbating in his bedroom by his mother. (Masturbating three to five times a week is pretty average among high school guys.) Lance's father just said, "That's my boy."

The reason I tell Lance's story is because he is where I see the *average* teenage male heading (though there is no way most parents will say Lance is the average). He was engaged in a few sexual relationships in high school, just like many other guys, but his appetite continued to grow stronger until he was consumed by it.

After making significant breakthroughs in counseling, Lance got married. He has been able to "come clean" to his wife about his secret life. They got help as a couple, and she learned ways to respond to him that would preserve their relationship. He has filters now and other tools to be successful in a monogamous relationship. He's basically had to create a brand-new thought pattern in regard to intimacy, love, and sex. He has his struggles, but when he faces those times he seeks support. Lance has also been courageous enough to talk to other young guys and give them the value of his experience, strength, and hope.

I tell you Lance's story to give *you* experience, strength, and hope. Experience in the evidence; this addiction stuff begins in consuming music videos, partaking in soft- or hard-core porn, and hooking up with girls in adolescence. Strength in that knowledge is power; you can impact your son's life early. And hope in the awareness that even when a kid falls into the trash can, a strong helping hand can pull him out. As parents, we just want to stop all this behavior — but kids need to grow, and they often grow only through painful experience. It may feel like we have no power as parents, but we really do — to forge a relationship, *no matter what.*

There Is Hope

Didn't Adam or Lance have any personal values? I hear this question every week as parents attempt to moralize their son's choices. My response is that everyone is reluctant to share internal personal conflict about sex, and everyone (a parent especially) is also reluctant to participate in processing the sexual experience. Guys just don't talk about it. They think it makes them look weak. We're not successful at telling them that it's not just about morals and values, but about relationships. Guys run the gamut from being cocky to being scared, but again, it's all about connection. In talking with them, a similar theme comes out: "If I had someone who could listen to me, help draw me out, challenge me to do the right thing, and *connect with me*, I really wouldn't have the need to just 'have sex.'"

I hope you're starting to feel something rise above the hopelessness and darkness of this subject. We are getting to the good news: *The past does not have to determine the future.*

Max, age seventeen, had been in the same relationship for

over a year. Max wanted to be intimate with his girlfriend but was scared because he thought he was overweight. "I don't have a great body," he told me. "She is just going to laugh at me." After he and his girlfriend did lose their virginity to each other, they decided that maybe they should have waited. "It's too complicated," Max told me. But a few weeks later he shared that they were having sex again.

"Why the change of heart?" I asked.

His answers: "We were bored; sex feels good; it's fun; it's connecting me to her in a way we have never connected before. It is also something new and exciting." You can hear his confusion and longing for a good relationship in every sentence. As I challenged him to think through his decision, he was convicted again about the importance of sex and the relationship, and he was *glad* that someone was asking tough questions like:

- Why do you feel the need to have sex to connect?
- Are there ways to connect aside from sex?
- How does sex really help you achieve your desire for personal (not just physical) intimacy?

These are tough questions that most kids *want* to think about. They also have a hard time answering them. If you can walk with them through this without inserting your own agenda at every turn, you may find them coming back to you as they continue to process.

Cameron came to see me when he was seventeen years old. His mom had died the previous December. He was an A/B student. He honestly confessed to me, "I think I'm in a situation that I might not be able to handle this weekend during prom." At my quizzical look he explained: "The girl is more into me than I am into her."

Sitting next to Cameron in my truck (we'd been to Subway for lunch), I asked, "What type of response are you looking for from me?"

With disarming honesty Cameron asked, "What would you do?"

I wanted to lecture: "Don't drink. Don't have sex." Instead we sat in the truck, and I asked questions. "Have you established any boundaries with her?"

"Whether we'll have sex, you mean?" Cameron asked.

"No. What do *you* feel comfortable with?" (We judge boys when we think all they want is sex. They want relationships as much as girls do.)

"Well, I'm not comfortable with sex," Cameron said quite confidently.

"Why?" I asked.

"That would be an abuse of power," this wise-beyond-his-years boy said, "because she likes me more than I like her."

Cameron had given himself his answer, but he still needed guidance as to how to live this out on a night when alcohol flows freely and hormones rage out of control. I shared with Cameron a story from my college swimming days. (Self-disclosure, shoulder to shoulder, can foster some of the most powerful connections.) I was a nationally ranked swimmer when I was in college, and one of my coaches was always setting higher and higher expectations for me. He would ask the team, "Who is ready to make the biggest deposit into the bank today, because

Nationals is coming. Who is going to make the biggest with-drawal at Nationals?" I would say, under my breath, "It's going to be me."

I explained to Cameron that he and his girlfriend had an unspoken contract that assumed they would have sex on prom night. I told him he needed to change the contract and allow his girlfriend to be a part of the process. It would be hard, but he needed to let her know that she had already made a greater emotional investment than he had. That investment may, in her eyes, allow her to make a big withdrawal. But, with less in the bank, he wasn't willing to make that withdrawal just yet. It symbolized something significant to him, and until his invest-ment matched that value, he would wait.

Cameron got it. My story confirmed his inner sense that taking something that didn't mean that much to him made him a "punk." Even more, the story also inspired him that there might be something out there (besides partying and hooking up) to invest in that would give him a truly valuable return.

Joining Our Sons' Stories

When I work with guys like Cameron or Max, I try to join them in their story. Joining does not mean that I am giving them permission to do dumb things. It means I'm empowering them and building on their autonomy. I join them by asking questions. I don't moralize. Sometimes I play the fool. I already know the answer, but they need to talk and emote and find their own truth. I am willing to tell my guys about mistakes I've made or about successes in my life. When I tell them about the times I've blown it, I tell them I'm not proud of it, but it probably needed to happen. Both failures and successes have created the story of who I am.

All too often parents shut down at this point because they don't think they're up to offering anything truly useful in the midst of the dilemmas their son faces. So they just moralize, which results in disconnection. Dads in particular will dissociate without ever stopping to think about what they're saying or doing. They model to their sons that when you are uncomfortable, dissociate and don't think. In order to make a connection, you're going to have to stop, ask questions, and join the story. It's irrational to believe that when we disconnect from our boys in the midst of what most interests or troubles them, they would have any interest in what we have to say when we are concerned or want to give them guidance.

Dads have a huge opportunity to connect with their sons in this area—especially to share their shortcomings. Sharing how you have "missed it" in terms of connection in relationships will impact your son *more* than the culture of high school. Be careful not to use these times as a trophy session—listing your conquests and notches. If you share how many women you slept with or how pretty they were, you will be encouraging your son to be like "all the other guys" out there. You will be giving him permission to roam the earth and devour as many women as he can in order to feel like a man.

Dads, could we take a moment and define what it means to be a man? Take three minutes and write out your top ten ideals of being a man. Does it include having sex with as many women as you can? Does it include justifying your behaviors so you can fit in with others? Does it include minimizing your behaviors because so-and-so has done worse than you? Probably not. In his book *Season of Life*, Jeffrey Marx reminds us how important our role is as fathers to our sons: "If you don't get some kind of a clear, compelling definition of masculinity at home, then you're pretty much left at the mercy of this society and the messages that are gonna speak to masculinity and manhood."[12]

When I ask guys to do this for a homework assignment (write out the top ten ideals for being a man), I almost always get a phone call halfway through the week. The response is often, "Man, am I ever blowing it in my life" or "Man, can I have any success in this area?" Young guys want to attach themselves to something of honor and respect. What's hard is that honor and respect are not highly touted values in high school. Getting lucky and getting wasted are.

A Word to Moms

Boys don't talk to their mothers about their sex lives. Why? Because it would crush Mom's heart. Moms, it really is that they don't want to disappoint you about this. They know that at some level moms can manage anger, substance abuse, bad grades, etc., but they can't micromanage sex because it begins and ends in the mind. This is different from the also-scary temptation of drugs and alcohol, because guys aren't experimenting with sex; they are having sex. It takes on a life of its own.

Moms, it's okay to talk to your sons about sex, but do so

with caution and wisdom. Be brief. Don't share your own sexual history. Boys don't need to hear this. They will lose total respect, even though they may say that they respect the girls in school who sleep around. You could disclose very generally, "I wasn't proud of how I handled myself in a few situations." But don't share too many stories because in the end you'll be judged. I know that sounds harsh, but it's true.

If a boy *is* talking a lot to his mom about sex, there's something off. He needs to be talking to a man. When a boy and his mother are having lots of conversations about his questions, experiences, and struggles with sex it connects them in a way that is confusing to a developing adolescent. If there is no dad in the picture, sell all that you have (I mean this) to find mentors, a youth pastor, or a counselor so that there will be a lot of male impact in this area. Boys like to be mentored by males who will ask them the tough questions like:

- What kind of story do you want to have when you're sitting with your future wife and you both go over your sexual history?
- What story do you want to have when your son asks you about your sexual history?

Most guys recognize the value in faithfulness, and therefore idealize someone who didn't sleep around. The problem is that trying to be a pure kid in a society that doesn't support purity is a difficult experience.

Some Thoughts for Dads

The best conversation I have with my guys about sex is when I talk about my wife. I tell them that I wasn't perfect, but God graciously kept me from having sex before I was married. When I talk about the woman I am married to and our family, I *always* cry. I tell guys that abstinence is not about keeping them from something; it's about preserving something. I am able to explain to my guys that I have a wonderful and passionate relationship with my wife. And it's not based on sex.

In their insecurity and immaturity most of them respond with, "Well, maybe you're not getting enough." What they need to hear is that a relationship is about so many other facets. I tell them there is something magical about being with a woman who knows what kind of toothpaste you like, and you don't want that level of intimacy with anyone else. Sometimes boys will roll their eyes, but they don't dismiss my tears, and many have mumbled, "Maybe you're on to something."

Most of my interactions with the guys I counsel on the subject of sex come about during shoulder-to-shoulder communication. We might be walking to the truck on our way for a burger, and I'll throw out a really heavy question, such as, "How are you doing with masturbation?" or "How much porn are your buddies into?" or "How are you dealing with the temptation to cross any lines sexually with your girlfriend?"

Their first reaction is "Fine." Translation: "Leave me alone." Their second reaction comes out of the shock to their system. They think, *Oh my gosh, I can't believe you just asked me that question!* And then they'll say, "You're kidding—you really want to know?" If there has been some groundwork, and I keep asking those questions, we end up taking that first step toward an avalanche — an outpouring that would bring a father and son closer together. In a dad's heart it might feel like an avalanche of destruction because he thinks, *I can't believe my son's been doing this.* But I have learned that when we totally freak out and shut down all communication, that's when all of the darkness and addiction grows. When things are lightly brought out into the light, boys relax and connect and are less likely to seek connection in all the wrong places.

So, dads, talk. Talk even though you feel uncomfortable. Do this during an activity — riding in the car, with your son's music on. Go get a Coke at 7-Eleven and maybe when you get back in the car comment on the provocative images you see on magazine covers. Find the smallest comment or question and work with that because it could turn into a major opportunity for you to connect with the heart of your son. Persevere, don't back down if your son shuts you down, and don't let fear keep you from pursuing him. Something small could turn into something huge. And then *the chase is on.*

GO FOR IT!

ON YOUR MARKS!

Purchase a computer program that will help you and your family know what is coming into your house — invited or uninvited — via the Internet. Programs change rapidly, so look online for the best software that monitors each and every keystroke of your son's cyber whereabouts. You can install the program or have a professional do it for you. The pros do a great job hiding the software if you choose not to tell your son at first that he is being monitored. Some teens are geniuses at coming up with ever more devious attempts to get around software that has been placed on the computer to help protect them and the family from unhealthy influences.

GET SET!

It is never too late to talk with your son about sex — remember that. Knowing that he is stimulated constantly by his culture can help you remember that sex is always on his mind — so it might as well be brought out into the light. Challenge yourself to come up with a list of twenty questions you can use to help protect and preserve him. For example, "What type of pressure do you feel to fit in sexually with the girls and guys you know?" or "If you could ask someone experienced anything at all about sex, what would it be?"

GO!

If you have a solid relationship with your spouse, advertise it frequently with your children. List each other's "top ten" relationship skills and talk about how important it is in your son's life to be practicing these kinds of skills to foster intimacy. Tell your son some *positive* things you remember about your own dating experience. For example, "When your dad and I were dating, I was so impressed when he would ask me how my day was or follow up on a miscommunication we'd had. He really showed he cared about me by doing that." Remember, you are the model — for better or worse — of how to relate to the opposite sex. Whether you realize it or not, your son is looking at you and to you to lead him to success in his future relationships.

8

A Crazy Little Thing Called Love

A few years ago I took a group of boys to climb in South America. We were standing at base camp looking at a magnificent mountain chain in the Andes. It had been cloudy, and when the clouds broke we saw for the first time the summits that we would climb. One of the guys looked with terror at those big mountains and said, "You want me to climb *that?*"

I think that's how teenagers feel as they see the challenges of growing up, and I know that's how parents of teenagers feel as they consider parenting them. I hope that in this book I have come alongside you in a way that supports you in the real world with your real son. I also hope you have caught a vision of the summit—a relationship that will outlast all of the awkwardness and awful moments that can come in growing up.

When we saw the peaks in South America and fear started to gnaw at the boys' hearts, I looked with them at the mountain range and said, "Isn't it going to be awesome!" I had a choice. I could have fueled their fear by saying, "Wow, we could totally die up there." But I wasn't going to live in fear. When they saw my confidence, they were ready to climb.

I tell boys and parents alike that there are no ninety-degree vertical mountains in the world. There are vertical sections that seem to go on and on, but there is no single mountain that is twenty thousand feet of sheer vertical ice and rock. The wind would simply blow it over.

Our families and our sons sometimes make us feel like we are climbing a sheer vertical face of discouragement, disappointment, and disconnection. It is my hope that this book has given you a few climbing tools to combat the temptation to stay "safe" on a snow shelf that at any moment may drop into an infinite crevasse. Staying put or being stuck is not an option. Why? Because your son's heart is at risk.

Ed Viesturs, the first American to climb all fourteen of the highest peaks in the world, said something about mountain climbing that I have found applies to pursuing the heart of a teenage boy: "I've learned in climbing that you don't 'conquer' anything. Mountains are not conquered and should be treated with respect and humility. If we take what the mountains give, have patience and desire, and are prepared, then the mountains will permit us to reach their highest peaks. I believe a lot of things are like that in life."[13]

Even when you are exposed to inclement bombardment, you can love your son exactly where he is. You can encourage his growth and you can feel good about the effort you are making, because when you allow your love for your son and your desire for a relationship to lead you, fear will not be a resting place. The journey may be hard, but it will also have awesome moments.

Once you catch and keep the vision for connection as the ultimate goal of parenting, you will be hooked—determined to find the keys to your son's heart.

Connecting the Dots

I receive a lot of desperate telephone calls from parents and frustrated calls from diversion officers (charged with steering first- or second-time youth offenders in the right direction) who are dealing with boys and young men who are acting out in some extreme and frightening ways. When I not only take their calls but express genuine interest in helping, they often ask me incredulously, "Would you really want to handle this kid?" My answer is always yes—even a kid who is acting out in the most extreme ways. When I am next asked, "How do you know?" I tell them what I believe—the premise of this book: "If I can *connect* with the kid, there is always hope." And connecting a lost boy to hope is a sacred privilege.

Perhaps you picked up this book with a heart full of fear or cynicism about parenting teenage boys. I hope that the information and stories you've read have helped you to connect the dots. The joy that you and I can experience as we dare to enter into our sons' world, understand the temptations and challenges they are facing, and try again and again to connect is worth all the bumps and bruises we may get along the way. The joy of watching a light come on in your son's face when someone else gets it is truly remarkable. That is why I come back to my office day after day to work with adolescent boys.

In the movie *The Rookie*, Jimmy Morris is a pitcher who enters the locker room, moves quickly to the other star player, and with a childlike and playful tone says to his friend, "Guess what we get to do today, Brooks?"

"Play baseball!"

Today and every day, you and I get to "Be parents!" Today is an important day to connect with your son. Perhaps not directly — but in every behavior, shining or terrifying, your son is asking for connection. He may be begging you for it. And I hope you are beginning to believe that you *can* — in fact, *only* you can — give him what he is so hungry for. It will take practicing consistent excitement, demonstrating sacrificial humility, and continuing to put one foot in front of the other.

Consistent Excitement

Teenagers don't choose behaviors in a vacuum. They are looking for connection — connection with you and with their own hearts. Sometimes the best way to open the door to connection is with an attitude of confidence or excitement about what the relationship with your son can be.

Do you remember the day your husband or wife told you that he or she loved you? Whether you screamed with excitement or your heart overflowed with a quiet confidence, just knowing that someone believed in you enough to profess such a convincing love changed who you were. Take that memory and well up with emotion; allow yourself to fall in love with your son because he desperately needs the light of your convincing belief in who he is and the assurance that you like him and are committed to him.

I am often asked how I can work with boys who are acting out with such extreme behaviors. Don't get me wrong. Some days are hard. I've had knives thrown at me, guns pulled on me, and swear words hurled at me, but I've remained passionate in my commitment to love and serve teens in trouble. I have no expectations that they will love me or serve me. I want them — and my own sons — to experience that I am just excited to be with them or near them.

How can parents maintain an attitude of consistent excitement when their sons are often awkward, withdrawn, or difficult to be with? First of all, we need to see what is most true about them, beyond their messy exteriors or scary behaviors.

Travis is a floppy-haired fifteen-year-old I've recently started working with. To say that he is gifted would be an understatement. However, due to daily pot smoking, he has watched his gifts be surpassed by those of his peers who are not living in a purple haze. In one of our sessions I broke down the neurochemical and physiological responses that his brain and body were going through as he smoked marijuana. Near the end of the session, it was as if a bright light went on inside Travis's head. His expression was priceless when he said, "That would explain my impulsivity and anger."

Most teenagers are desperate to understand themselves, but they do not have the capacity to do so fully. It is our job to help our child discover the person we know him to be. That means we need to understand their world and the challenges they face while we hold on to the memory of who they really are. I told Travis about the consequences of smoking pot — not because

I wanted to guilt or shame him into stopping, but because I wanted him to remember who he is. I said to him, "You just thought you were an angry, out-of-control kid, but that's not who you *really* are." Relief filled his face and heart.

You may be tempted to dismiss self-discovery and identity development as psychobabble, but I have discovered that knowing who you are is essential to spiritual transformation and healthy emotional development. We all search for a way to be comfortable in our own skin. It is our job as parents to connect the dots for our sons and continually call them back from destructive behaviors to their unique gifts, talents, and longing for connection. If we can help our boys find their true selves, they will be more likely to find God and seek out healthy human relationships.

Hard work? Absolutely. That is why a second principle in maintaining consistent excitement about your son is so important. We must *take care of ourselves* or there is no way we can handle this task of heroic proportions. As we connect the dots for our sons, we must stay focused on not personalizing their behavior. We have looked at this throughout the book, but I want to reemphasize that loving your son well means you can't take his behaviors personally. I don't know how you can rise to this challenge unless you maintain your own health—physically, emotionally, and spiritually.

Moms, in particular, think they need to throw themselves under the bus in order to love. That's not love. That is being a martyr, and your son doesn't need a martyr; he needs a strong, confident parent. Often a boy's response to a martyr mom will be to say, "I'm out of here." It is too much pressure for him to bear.

If you are a single parent who has made extraordinary efforts to put family first, I have to remind you that you are the most important person in the equation of what it takes to raise a healthy son. Finding even five minutes for yourself may seem next to impossible, but try incorporating a ten-minute walk on your work break. Meet a friend for lunch so you can get out what is on your heart. Schedule your Saturday around a few things that are important to you.

Now is the time for you to evaluate how well you are caring for yourself. Sometimes when you are in crisis with a child, it's hard to believe that taking care of yourself is essential to fuel you to love your son, but it is. Parents who have never developed a consistent pattern of caring for themselves will be limited in the love they can demonstrate to their children.

If this is your experience and you are feeling tired and burned out, hear this as an invitation, not a reprimand. Don't allow yourself to be distracted by discouragement or guilt. As you give yourself permission to make time for yourself, you will discover you have a greater capacity to be excited about parenting.

Sacrificial Humility

When you are focused on what is most true about your son and committed to caring for yourself, you will begin to act out of sacrificial humility. Sacrificial humility can look different for every child and parent. When I receive a crisis intervention phone call, I often have to refocus parents who are scared or at their wits' end. I remind myself and them—often while I hear swearing and things being slammed in the background—of the true goal, which is connecting with their son. Sometimes that means you have to find a distraction from the fight of the day or the crisis of the moment. I know that can be hard because often the crisis seems like the most important thing in the world or the only thing in the world.

I got just such a crisis phone call from one distraught mom. In the middle of her distress I asked her, "What did you have for lunch today?" She replied with predictable surprise and a little irritation, "What are you talking about?" I explained that I was trying to take her focus off the immediate events so that she could slow down, problem-solve, and even change directions. This takes humility, because when faced with a crisis we often feel justified in going full-steam ahead. The problem is that we may lose our children along the way.

This mom learned from my interruption and began to practice this with her son when he became belligerent or frustrated. She began to distract her son from the angst of the moment by asking, "Did I leave the oven on?" or some other inane question. She discovered that a little redirection allowed both her and her son to cool down and be more available for connection.

Sometimes being humble means we let down our defenses. I worked with one family where the dad was often away from home because of his work. When he began to see that his son's acting out was really begging for him to be available for a relationship, he began to find ways to be at home more. He was a bit chagrined when, during a recent outburst, his son exclaimed, "The reason I am doing so bad in school is because you have not been there for me!" This dad wanted to defend himself and go down his internal list of how he had changed and all the ways he had been there for his son recently, but because he knew that his son's expression came out of a desire for relationship, and because he had taken time to evaluate himself and care for himself, he was able to answer, "I know I haven't been there for you as much as I should have been, but that is changing, and I am committed to being there for you in the future."

To his surprise his son began to cry. He asked him, "What's wrong?" His son replied, "I just needed you to say that." Because this dad was vulnerable, his son was able to be vulnerable as well—and that is the context for the most powerful connection!

When we become defensive or rehearse our checklist of all that we've done, we create a context for kids to shut down. When teenagers, in particular, experience our defensiveness on a regular basis, it becomes almost impossible to reel them back into relationship.

Humility also includes a willingness to look for something positive in the midst of overwhelming negative circumstances. Jonathan is seventeen years old and comes from a difficult background. He is being raised by his mom and has severed his relationship with his dad due to physical and emotional abuse. Jonathan's mom has faced enormous challenges in parenting him. As is often the case when a child is abused, he reenacted that abuse in self-destructive behaviors. He was failing school and ready to drop out.

Jonathan called me recently, and in the midst of a lot of anxiety and anger I found a flicker of hope. At the end of his tirade Jonathan asked, "Well, what do *you* think I should do?" Hope welled up within me, because I knew that Jonathan was asking for help. I was careful not to pounce on him with all my advice and opinions. I began by saying, "Man, I am so honored that you care what I think." My humility kept the conversation going and the connection alive. Seeing something positive fueled my own excitement for Jonathan, and that enthusiasm became contagious as we conversed. Jonathan expressed a willingness to enroll at an alternative school and finish his education or pursue a GED. All because I honored him for asking for help? Absolutely. Teenagers are desperate for someone to believe in them—especially when they are in the midst of flailing and failing.

Jonathan's mom was ready to take him to this alternative school without contempt or complaint. A lot of parents quit when it gets hard, and then boys will act out even more. They quit as well. I know that teenage boys can wear parents down. Humility is a commitment to invite again, suggest again, believe again, and forgive again — *to dwell in the possibilities.*

I know that for you single moms sacrifice is a daily reality. I think I understand a little more of what you are going through today than I did a few months ago. At the time of this writing, my wife is pregnant with our fourth child and is horribly sick. I am juggling a busy counseling practice while trying to be Mr. Mom to help her out. I find myself wanting to collapse in tears at the end of the day. So let me say thank you to you single moms (and dads) for your commitment. Your son may seem disconnected from your sacrifice right now, but you are modeling something to him that will serve him throughout his life. Although I feel like collapsing at the end of the day, I don't feel sorry for myself. I know that being present to my children, being committed to my family, and sacrificing for my spouse and kids is not something bad for me; rather, it is contributing to my own growth as I serve them. I am asking for a heart of gratitude for the privilege of offering sacrificial love.

Putting One Foot in Front of the Other

During our honeymoon my wife and I participated in a five-day trek on the border of northern Thailand. At the end of the trek there was a mile-long walk through a bat cave. This cave was not only filled with thousands and thousands of bats, but there were also pit vipers along the way. We were guided by one man with a headlamp. As we walked, it felt like the cave was closing in on us, getting darker and darker. I could feel the pressure of the bats brush the top of my head. But we got through that cave by putting one foot in front of the other.

I often think of that mile-long trek when I think about parenting. Some days are tunnel-walking days, when it feels like the best you can do is put one foot in front of the other. If you keep walking, however, you *will* eventually see light at the other end of the tunnel. Our responsibility is to lean on those who are ahead of us and to turn to those behind us and encourage them, "Keep walking. There is light ahead."

There is no denying that parenting is hard work. But I have worked with enough boys—many of them in the most extreme situations—to know that there is light ahead as long as we keep the goal of connecting ever before us. That is where this crazy little thing called love comes in. I have discovered that it really is the power of love that pulls us forward.

But just as our sons' behaviors don't occur in a vacuum, our love does not grow in a vacuum, either. We cannot do this alone. I have found that moms are more likely to form support groups, share their struggles, and pray with other moms. Dads, we need support, too, if we are going to love our sons well.

Don owns his own computer software company and travels weekly. He has a staff of seventy-five people, and he bragged about making an exorbitant living—often $200,000 per month. He is a global jet-setter and has a passion for his corporation. He came in to see me after his son, Justin, had been in counseling for four months. He wanted me to know that he had seen some growth but felt that Justin had a long way to go to be the best young man possible. He asked me what more I was going to do to bring about change in his son.

In my initial response I focused on the relationship I had developed with Justin. I told Don that his son trusted me and had developed and was implementing a plan for personal integrity, character, sobriety, and intimate relationships. I then turned the question back to him by asking, "What are *you* doing to help him with this plan?" He was shocked. "That's what I pay you for," he barked. I responded by saying that he had a critical role to play—that the best way to encourage growth and change in his son was to *pursue him* and spend time with him.

Don dropped his head. Staring at the floor, he was honest in his response. "I don't think my son likes me much," he said. "I don't even know how to talk with him. I only know how to talk at him."

Two weeks later Don accepted my invitation to join me in the field for a day of climbing and personal coaching with a group of ninth and tenth graders whom I had never met. I was asked to lead these at-risk youth in an experiential activity (I chose rock climbing) and make some parallels to their lives that might encourage growth and change for them. Throughout the exercise I pointed out and encouraged their physical and behavioral strengths. The young men responded enthusiastically. After completing the climbing, I asked each of them to verbalize some parallels of what we'd done physically to each of their emotional worlds. I got a bunch of blank stares followed by a lot of heads dropping as the guys looked at the ground. I knew what was going on. They felt confused and uncomfortable. They had not done an exercise like this before and they were untrained in how to respond.

The following day I took twelve of my regular clients in the same age group to the same location for the same exercise. Don and a couple of other fathers came along and participated with their sons. At the end of our time together I asked my clients the same questions I had asked the boys I had never worked with. The responses from my clients were deep, from-the-heart, and well paralleled to their struggles and hopes and dreams for change.

I noticed the fathers looking at me like, *Holy cow! Where did that come from?* They were not used to seeing their sons communicate like this. I then asked the fathers to respond to what their sons said. There was not a dry eye among them as they celebrated their sons' efforts and growth.

On the way down the trail Don asked to walk with me for a minute. He, too, was in a process of making some connections in regard to what he'd observed over the past two days. He asked me why I asked him to come to both outings. I told him

I'd wanted him to see for himself the difference between the kids who had not had any modeling of what it means to really participate in communication and growth (because no one had come alongside them to show them how) and my clients, who have gotten it in their heads that when I ask them personal questions, it is acceptable and expected that they will participate and show up for me because I have proven to them that I will show up for them.

Don started to weep. We ended up sitting on a rock together for over an hour, talking about what his desires for connecting with his son and wife really looked like for him. A month later Don came in for a session, asking for help in restructuring his priorities so his family would come first. His extreme dream was to connect with his son, so we began putting in place strategies for how he could do his part in making this dream come true. Don is fortunate that he could afford to scale back his work. That gave him a starting point. He limited himself to a forty-hour workweek, which he stuck to for the next eighteen months while he worked his tail off in countless individual and family therapy sessions.

Don recently called to thank me for saving him from himself and for saving his family. I thanked him for the trust he had placed in me to lead his family toward healing. Most important I assured him that their success was due in large part to his willingness to be humble about his disconnection with everyone around him. From this place of humility Don was able to access the courage and commitment he needed to put one foot in front of the other in an extreme pursuit that led him to the summit of what he'd thought was unattainable.

I tell every person in my practice that life is like a mountain. We all have summits we don't feel like we can reach. In my mind, pursuing connection is the single greatest gift we can give to our sons and to ourselves. Even if we don't make it to the top—and a lot of times we won't—life is all about the pursuit, and our success is measured by every step we are willing to take. When we choose to put our hearts on the line for the sake of our sons, we offer them the thing they crave the most. And then *the chase is on.*

GO FOR IT!

ON YOUR MARKS!

Write down your son's gifts, personality traits, character qualities, and talents so you can keep a vision of who he is beyond his messy room, mediocre grades, or foolish behaviors. Then get into the habit of taking this a step further by letting your son know that you recognize what is good about him. Write him a short note, send him a text message, or compliment him to his face. You might be amazed at how little it takes to start connecting with him.

GET SET!

Make a list of five episodes within the past six months in which you found yourself overreacting to your son. What set you off? Next list five tools you have learned about in this book that could help you to stay present for your son in the midst of your next conflict. Keep the list in your wallet or purse, in your day planner, or on the inside of a cabinet door. If you get into the habit of reviewing this list often, you will be less likely to revert to your old habits. Most important, you will show your son that you can be present and focused, even though you may be freaking out on the inside.

GO!

What are three things you need to do to take better care of yourself? Make a commitment to do all three *this week*. Feeling better about yourself will help you feel better about the people around you. If you do not take care of yourself you will not have what it takes to pursue the heart of your son. You are both worth it!

Acknowledgments

To my bride: Thank you for encouraging me to write this book. Thank you for loving me. You are an amazing woman. I love watching you as a mom. You are my everything.

Mom, you bless me with the very presence of being a huge part of my life. You have championed me with every prayer on every day, even at four in the morning when I was adrift. Thank you for loving me when I was unlovable and unlikable.

Dad, you have been my guide and coach. You have loved me and taught me what integrity looks like. Thank you for loving Mom so much.

2xtreme families, thank you for trusting me with your sons' hearts and lives. Thank you for working so hard.

2xtreme young men, I love you all and am so blessed to have been taught and touched by your stories, excitement, struggles, and joys. Most importantly, thank you for trusting me with your journey! May you all continue to climb even when storms roll in.

Sharon Hersh (my dear friend and colleague), thank you for all that you have done to make this dream a reality. I could not have done this without you. Thank you for believing in me. Your support and encouragement have been invaluable.

Traci Mullins (my editor), thank you so much for being such a wonderful project manager. Navigating my every move with encouragement and strength. Your expertise and experience refined this project beyond what I could have imagined!

Don Pape, thank you for pursuing me to do this project and encouraging me to share my heart.

NavPress, thank you for believing in the relationship of fathers and sons.

Appendix

How to Spot Substance Abuse in Your Son

Being a student of your son could save his life when it comes to noticing the signs and symptoms of drug and alcohol use or abuse. The following list will help you pay attention to the changes in his behavior. If you have questions and/or concerns, *never* hesitate to consult with your primary-care physician or local licensed drug and alcohol treatment facility. For a list of licensed treatment facilities go to www.findtreatment.samhsa.gov.

MARIJUANA

In their book *Teens Under the Influence*, Katherine Ketcham and Nicholas Pace outline the following signs and symptoms as closely linked to continuous marijuana use.

Problems at Home
- Withdrawal from family activities.
- Arguing with siblings and parents.
- Acting sullen or uncommunicative.
- Refusing to do chores, homework.

- Routinely breaking house rules such as meeting curfews, using appropriate language, being respectful of others.

Physical Signs
- Unusual or chronic fatigue.
- Clacking sound when talking.
- Lips stick to teeth.
- Dry mouth.
- Chapped lips.
- Never-ending smile.
- Red, bloodshot eyes.
- Squinty eyes.
- Dilated pupils.

Emotional/Mental Problems
- Anxiety.
- Depression, mild or severe.
- Mood swings.
- Hostility.
- Sudden anger.
- Memory lapses.

Problems at School
- Teachers complain about your child's attitude or behavior in class.
- Low motivation.
- Apathy about school performance.
- Grades begin to drop.
- Absenteeism.
- Truancy.

- Loss of interest in sports or other extracurricular activities.

Behavior Changes

- Carelessness with clothing, hairstyle, or makeup.
- Desire to be with new friends.
- Frequent overnights at other people's houses.
- Excessive laughter or giggling over silly or trivial events.
- Signs of drugs and drug paraphernalia, including pipes and rolling papers.
- Odor on clothes and in the bedroom.
- Use of incense and other deodorizers.
- Use of eyedrops, breath mints, chewing gum, mouthwash.
- Music, clothing, posters, or jewelry promoting drug use.
- Excessive hunger, overeating, or feasting on high-sugar and high-fat foods. [14]

CENTRAL NERVOUS SYSTEM DEPRESSANTS

Alcohol

Physical Signs of Alcohol Intoxication

It is important to note that the level of intoxication can directly affect the intensity of the signs and symptoms of alcohol use. According to The Partnership for a Drug-Free America's website, any of the following could be a sign of intoxication:

- Slurred speech or difficulty expressing a thought intelligibly
- Lack of coordination, poor balance
- Can't walk a straight line
- Can't focus on your eyes
- Red eyes or flushed face
- Morning headaches, nausea, weakness, or sweatiness
- Odor of alcohol on breath or in sweat[15]

Other Signs of Alcohol Use

According to the helpguide.org website, there are other signs of alcohol use you should be aware of:

Alcohol is the number one drug of choice among young people. Teens consume more alcohol than all the other illicit drugs combined. . . .

Certain warning signs indicate that your child may have a drinking problem. One or two of the following signs are common in all children, especially teens, as they are adjusting to the bodily and social changes that are a part of their stage of life. It is advisable to have a talk with your child, however, if you notice several of the following signs:

- The odor of alcohol
- Sudden change in mood or attitude
- Change in attendance or performance at school
- Loss of interest in school, sports, or other activities
- Discipline problems at school

- Withdrawal from family and friends
- Secrecy
- Association with a new group of friends and reluctance to introduce them to you
- Alcohol disappearing from your home
- Depression and developmental difficulties[16]

DESIGNER DRUGS

Ecstasy (MDMA)

Ecstasy is an orally ingested central nervous system stimulant that primarily affects serotonin, a chemical in your brain responsible for mood stability.

Signs of Ecstasy Use

- Excessive water consumption
- Teeth grinding
- Chills, sweating
- Mood swings
- Slurred speech
- Hangover symptoms: nausea, vomiting, and headaches
- Poor memory and lack of focus
- Sporadic academic performance
- Depression
- Dehydration
- Memory loss
- Anxiety

Ecstasy Basics

There is a huge misconception among teens that ecstasy is not a drug that will harm them, with the result that one in nine teenagers has tried the drug.[17] The U.S. Department of Health and Human Services put together the following list to aid you in determining if your teen is using ecstasy.

- The drug makes the body less able to control its temperature and water content, most often putting users at risk of overheating and dehydration.
- Use of ecstasy can increase a person's heart rate and blood pressure.
- Ecstasy can cause tension in the jaw and an urge to chew and clench one's teeth.
- For days after taking ecstasy, a person may feel depressed and slow.
- Those who use ecstasy may have trouble with short-term memory and may find it hard to focus their thoughts.
- Ecstasy users can't be sure how strong a dose of ecstasy is.
- Ecstasy use carries added risks since other drugs may be mixed with ecstasy, sometimes without a user's knowledge.
- Studies are being done to find out more about the long-term effects of ecstasy on the brain.[18]

HALLUCINOGENS

- Extremely dilated pupils
- Warm skin
- Excessive perspiration
- Body odor
- Distorted sense of sight, hearing, touch
- Distorted image of self and time
- Mood and behavior changes
- Hallucinations
- Depersonalization
- Paranoia
- Depression[19]

STIMULANTS

Cocaine

Stimulants are very dangerous and highly addictive substances. You can find valuable resources at www.adolescent-substance-abuse.com, such as the following list of the signs and symptoms of cocaine use:

- Dilated (large) pupils
- Hyper-alertness
- Lack of fatigue/sleeplessness
- Panic and/or heightened anxiety response
- Restlessness

- Paranoia (high doses)
- Extremely talkative; fast speech
- Runny nose or bloody nose
- Seizures (high doses; bad reaction)
- White powder seen on face or clothes
- Small spoon-like items used for snorting
- Mirrors and razor blades used for making lines
- Rolled money bills used for snorting
- Small bottles with screw on lids for storing
- Small plastic packets with white residue[20]

Methamphetamines

Another great resource, www.stopmeth.com, lists the following among many other signs and symptoms of methamphetamine use:

- Increased alertness (mania)
- Sense of well-being
- Paranoia
- Panic
- Aggressive/violent behavior
- Increased heart rate
- Convulsions
- Extreme rise in body temperature (as high as 108 degrees, which can cause brain damage and death)
- Uncontrollable movements (twitching, jerking, etc.)
- Insomnia

- Impaired speech
- Acne, sores
- Weight loss
- Moodiness and irritability
- Rotting teeth
- Disturbed sleep[21]

Notes

1. Patricia Hersch, *A Tribe Apart: A Journey into the Heart of American Adolescence* (New York: Balantine, 1998), 71.
2. Ron Taffel, *The Second Family: Reckoning with Adolescent Power* (New York: St. Martin, 2001), 118.
3. Sharon A. Hersh, *"Mom, Everyone Else Does!"* (Colorado Springs, CO: Shaw Books, 2005), 14.
4. U.S. Department of Justice, *Bureau of Justice Statistics*, 2002 (Washington, DC: Government Printing Office, 2002), NCJ 194449.
5. Terrence Real, *I Don't Want to Talk About It* (New York: Scribner, 1997), 127.
6. Sharon A. Hersh, *"Mom, Sex Is No Big Deal!"* (Colorado Springs, CO: Shaw Books, 2006), 16.
7. Robert Shaw, *The Epidemic: The Rot of American Culture, Absentee and Permissive Parenting, and the Resultant Plague of Joyless, Selfish Children* (New York: HarperCollins, 2003), 18.
8. Hersh, *"Mom, Sex Is No Big Deal!"*, 16.

9. Centers for Disease Control and Prevention, "Sexual Risk Behaviors," *Healthy Youth!*, January 11, 2007. http://www.cdc.gov/healthyyouth/sexualbehaviors/index.htm.

10. 2002 National Survey of Family Growth, cited in U.S. Department of Health and Human Services, Centers for Disease Control and Prevention, "Teenagers in the United States: Sexual Activity, Contraceptive Use, and Childbearing, 2002," *Vital and Health Statistics* 23, no. 24 (December 2004), table 3, http://www.cdc.gov/nchs/data/series/sr_23/sr23_024.pdf.

11. National Coalitation for the Protection of Children and Families, "Pornography," http://www.nationalcoalition.org/resourcesservices/stat.html.

12. Jeffrey Marx, *Season of Life* (New York: Simon & Schuster, 2003), 71.

13. Ed Viesturs with David Roberts, *No Shortcuts to the Top* (New York: Broadway Books, 2006), 302.

14. Katherine Ketcham and Nicholas A. Pace, MD, *Teens Under the Influence* (New York: Ballantine, 2003), 120–121.

15. "Signs of Abuse Related to Particular Substances," The Partnership for a Drug-Free America, June 6, 2006. http://www.drugfree.org/Intervention/Articles/Signs_of_abuse.

16. John Dorsey, Heather Larson, and Jeanne Segal, PhD, "Alcohol Abuse and Alcoholism: Signs, Symptoms, Effects, and Testing," Helpguide.org, January 27, 2007. http://www.helpguide.org/mental/alcohol_abuse_alcoholism_signs_effects_treatment.htm#alcohol_abuse_alcoholism_signs_symptoms.

17. U.S. Department of Health and Human Services and SAMHSA's National Clearinghouse for Alcohol and Drug Information, "Ecstasy: Parents Need to Check In," *Prevention Alert* 6, no. 13 (2003), http://ncadi.samhsa.gov/govpubs/prevalert/v6/13.aspx.

18. U.S. Department of Health and Human Services, "Survey Shows Parents Need Facts About Ecstasy," *Family Guide*, http://family.samhsa.gov/monitor/parentsurvey.aspx.

19. "Detailed Signs and Symptoms of Drug Use," *Employee Assistance*, February 10, 2006, http://eap.partners.org/WorkLife/Addiction/Kids_and_drugs/Signs_and_Symptoms_of_Drug_Use.asp.

20. "Recognizing Use: Cocaine and/or Crack," *Adolescent Substance Abuse Knowledge Base*, http://www.adolescent-substance-abuse.com/signs-cocaine.html.

21. "What Are the Signs and Symptoms of Methamphetamine Use?" Stop Meth, http://www.stopmeth.com/signs.htm.

About the Author

JOHN E. DAVIS holds a clinical master's degree in counseling psychology and is also a certified addictions counselor. He works primarily with at-risk adolescents and their families and has counseled well over one thousand boys over the past twelve years. The Drug and Alcohol Abuse Division for the State of Colorado nominated John's drug and alcohol program as Program of the Year for 2002. Network and cable affiliates in the Denver area have featured John's work with adolescents, and he has been honored with the Channel 4 News Hometown Hero Award. More information about his counseling practice is available at www.2xtreme.info. John is a sought-after speaker for high schools and universities, postgraduate programs, businesses, youth organizations, and churches. He and his wife, Valerie, live in Denver with their four children.

MORE PARENTING HELP FROM NAVPRESS.

Parenting with Love and Logic

Foster Cline, MD, and Jim Fay

ISBN-13: 978-1-57683-954-6   ISBN-10: 1-57683-954-0

Parents have only a few years to prepare their children for a world that requires responsibility and maturity for survival. *Parenting with Love and Logic* helps parents raise healthy, responsible kids. Recently revised and updated.

Parenting Teens with Love and Logic

Foster Cline, MD, and Jim Fay

ISBN-13: 978-1-57683-930-0   ISBN-10: 1-57683-930-3

You don't have to dread the teenage years! Learn how to parent your teens without nagging or yelling and prepare them for a responsible adulthood. Recently revised and updated.

Respectful Kids

Dr. Todd Cartmell

ISBN-13: 978-1-57683-984-3   ISBN-10: 1-57683-984-2

Family coach and child psychologist Dr. Todd Cartmell offers you a proven three-part strategy that can transform family relationships through the power of respect. Not only will these techniques strengthen your family, they'll prepare your children for godly maturity and successful relationships in adulthood.

To order copies, visit your local Christian bookstore,
call NavPress at 1-800-366-7788, or log on to www.navpress.com.
To locate a Christian bookstore near you, call 1-800-991-7747.

NAVPRESS®
BRINGING TRUTH TO LIFE
www.navpress.com